ABORTION

OPPOSING VIEWPOINTS®

Other Books of Related Interest

Why Consider Opposing Viewpoints?

"The only way in which a human being can make some approach to knowing the whole of a subject is by hearing what can be said about it by persons of every variety of opinion and studying all modes in which it can be looked at by every character of mind. No wise man ever acquired his wisdom in any mode but this."

John Stuart Mill

In our media-intensive culture it is not difficult to find differing opinions. Thousands of newspapers and magazines and dozens of radio and television talk shows resound with differing points of view. The difficulty lies in deciding which opinion to agree with and which "experts" seem the most credible. The more inundated we become with differing opinions and claims, the more essential it is to hone critical reading and thinking skills to evaluate these ideas. Opposing Viewpoints books address this problem directly by presenting stimulating debates that can be used to enhance and teach these skills. The varied opinions contained in each book examine many different aspects of a single issue. While examining these conveniently edited opposing views, readers can develop critical thinking skills such as the ability to compare and contrast authors' credibility, facts, argumentation styles, use of persuasive techniques, and other stylistic tools. In short, the Opposing Viewpoints Series is an ideal way to attain the higher-level thinking and reading skills so essential in a culture of diverse and contradictory opinions.

In addition to providing a tool for critical thinking, Opposing Viewpoints books challenge readers to question their own strongly held opinions and assumptions. Most people form their opinions on the basis of upbringing, peer pressure, and personal, cultural, or professional bias. By reading carefully balanced opposing views, readers must directly confront new ideas as well as the opinions of those with whom they disagree. This is not to simplistically argue that everyone who reads opposing views will—or should—change his or her opinion. Instead, the series enhances readers' understanding of their own views by encouraging confrontation with opposing ideas. Careful examination of others' views can lead to the readers' understanding of the logical inconsistencies in their own opinions, perspective on why they hold an opinion, and the consideration of the possibility that their opinion requires further evaluation.

Evaluating Other Opinions

To ensure that this type of examination occurs, Opposing Viewpoints books present all types of opinions. Prominent spokespeople on different sides of each issue as well as well-known professionals from many disciplines challenge the reader. An additional goal of the series is to provide a forum for other, less known, or even unpopular viewpoints. The opinion of an ordinary person who has had to make the decision to cut off life support from a terminally ill relative, for example, may be just as valuable and provide just as much insight as a medical ethicist's professional opinion. The editors have two additional purposes in including these less known views. One, the editors encourage readers to respect others' opinions—even when not enhanced by professional credibility. It is only by reading or listening to and objectively evaluating others' ideas that one can determine whether they are worthy of consideration. Two, the inclusion of such viewpoints encourages the important critical thinking skill of objectively evaluating an author's credentials and bias. This evaluation will illuminate an author's reasons for taking a particular stance on an issue and will aid in readers' evaluation of the author's ideas.

It is our hope that these books will give readers a deeper understanding of the issues debated and an appreciation of the complexity of even seemingly simple issues when good and honest people disagree. This awareness is particularly important in a democratic society such as ours in which people enter into public debate to determine the common good. Those with whom one disagrees should not be regarded as enemies but rather as people whose views deserve careful examination and may shed light on one's own.

Thomas Jefferson once said that "difference of opinion leads to inquiry, and inquiry to truth." Jefferson, a broadly educated man, argued that "if a nation expects to be ignorant and free . . . it expects what never was and never will be." As individuals and as a nation, it is imperative that we consider the opinions of others and examine them with skill and discernment. The Opposing Viewpoints Series is intended to help readers achieve this goal.

David L. Bender and Bruno Leone,
Founders

Greenhaven Press anthologies primarily consist of previously published material taken from a variety of sources, including periodicals, books, scholarly journals, newspapers, government documents, and position papers from private and public organizations. These original sources are often edited for length and to ensure their accessibility for a young adult audience. The anthology editors also change the original titles of these works in order to clearly present the main thesis of each viewpoint and to explicitly indicate the opinion presented in the viewpoint. These alterations are made in consideration of both the reading and comprehension levels of a young adult audience. Every effort is made to ensure that Greenhaven Press accurately reflects the original intent of the authors included in this anthology.

Introduction

"[Constitutionally protected] abortion . . . has never been understood . . . to include taking the life of a partly born child."

—*U.S. Catholic Conference*

"A criminal statute banning any medically safe method of abortion unduly infringes upon women's rights."

—*Abortion Access Project*

Abortion is one of the most persistently controversial issues in American culture and politics today. Since the 1973 national legalization of abortion, competing groups have fought to either restrict or increase access to the procedure, leading to heated debates among political activists, religious organizations, state legislatures, and judges.

This conflict is perhaps reflective of the nation's ambivalence over abortion. While it is often depicted as a two-sided debate, the abortion controversy is actually quite multifaceted, involving complex speculation on biology, ethics, and constitutional rights. Those who identify themselves as pro-life, for example, generally contend that abortion is wrong because it kills human life, which they believe begins at conception. However, some pro-lifers grant that abortion should be allowed in cases of rape or incest, or when the pregnancy threatens the life or health of the mother. Those who identify themselves as pro-choice often maintain that abortion must remain legal because a woman should have the right to control her body and her destiny. But some pro-choicers also believe that there should be certain restrictions on teen access to abortion and on abortions occurring after the first trimester of pregnancy. This mixture of opinions is probably why Gallup polls consistently show that 50 to 60 percent of Americans favor abortion "only under certain circumstances."

The continuing debate over a relatively new form of second-trimester abortion called intact dilation and extraction (D&X) reveals the complexity of American opinion on the subject. Referred to as "partial-birth abortion" by its opponents, D&X is usually performed on women who are between twenty and twenty-four weeks pregnant, ostensibly when the fetus has severe defects or when the pregnancy endangers the mother's health. During the procedure, the doctor delivers all but the head of the fetus from the uterus, then uses scissors to cut a hole in the base of the fetus's skull so that its contents can be removed. This allows the fetus's head to collapse so that it can more easily pass through the cervical opening.

Opponents of D&X maintain that it is a grisly and immoral procedure akin to infanticide. At twenty-four weeks, they contend, more than 50 percent of fetuses are potentially viable (able to survive outside of the womb). Moreover, as Illinois physicians M. LeRoy Sprang and Mark G. Neerhoff claim, the procedure is hardly ever performed as a result of a medical emergency: "The vast majority [are] done not in response to extreme medical conditions but on healthy mothers and healthy fetuses." They point out that 56 percent of partial-birth abortions are done as a result of "fetal flaws . . . some as minor as a cleft lip," while 9 percent involve maternal health problems, "of which the most common [is] depression."

Abortion-rights supporters assert that the vast majority of abortions are performed in the first trimester, with only 1.4 percent occurring after twenty-one weeks of pregnancy: approximately two thousand per year. Some contend that the furor over a relatively rare procedure, which became a focal point for anti-abortion activism in the 1990s, was at heart an attempt to sway public opinion against the more common types of abortion. However, most of the physicians who perform D&X abortions grant that the majority of such procedures are elective and not medically necessary.

These revelations about the D&X procedure disquieted Americans on all sides of the debate. *New York Times* polls taken in 1997 concluded that between 54 and 71 percent of Americans opposed late-term abortions. However, another 1997 poll commissioned by the Republican Coalition for Choice found that 82 percent of the public believed that the D&X option is a "medical decision that should be made by a woman, her doctor, her family, and her clergy." These seemingly contradictory poll results reflect public distaste over the procedure as well as a reluctance to cede individual rights, claims Coalition for Choice president Susan R. Cullman: "People say, 'It's an awful procedure. I can't stand it. Get rid of it.' But when you say, 'If you're in this predicament, do you want doctors to give you options?' the answer is, 'Of course.'"

The D&X procedure did not exist in 1973, when the Supreme Court's *Roe v. Wade* decision held that a woman's right to privacy—including the right to choose to end a pregnancy in the first two trimesters—was protected by the Fourteenth Amendment. However, the Court's 1992 decision in *Planned Parenthood v. Casey* did allow states to set certain kinds of limits on access to abortions. Under *Casey*, as long as no "undue burden" is placed on women seeking abortions, states can regulate access to the procedure. As a result, many state legislatures enforced restrictions on abortion, including laws that significantly limited or banned the D&X procedure. In addition, between 1995 and 2000, Congress passed several bills attempting to impose a nationwide ban on D&X abortions—although each of these bills was vetoed by President Bill Clinton.

In June 2000, in a 5-to-4 decision, the U.S. Supreme Court struck down a Nebraska ban on partial-birth abortions. Justice Stephen Breyer argued that the state's law was unconstitutional because it did not include any exceptions for protecting the health of the mother and because the overly vague language of the law could have been used to ban the more common types of second-trimester abortions. The ruling leaves open, however, the possibility that a more clearly defined D&X ban could some day gain the approval of the Court.

The complex ethical and legal debate over abortion shows no sign of abating as activists, legislators, and judges continue to ponder if and when the procedure should be regulated. *Abortion: Opposing Viewpoints* explores this and several other contentious issues in the following chapters: Is Abortion Immoral? Should Abortion Rights Be Restricted? Can Abortion Be Justified? Is Abortion Safe? The authors in this anthology present compelling arguments concerning the morality, accessibility, purpose, and effect of abortion.

CHAPTER 1

Is Abortion Immoral?

Chapter Preface

One of the most controversial issues of the abortion debate is the question of when human life begins. Many abortion opponents argue that life commences at the moment of conception, when a sperm fertilizes an egg cell. Fertilization, they contend, creates a unique individual with a complete genetic code that is separate from that of its mother. Consequently, terminating a pregnancy kills an innocent and defenseless human being, anti-abortionists maintain. As pro-life lawyers Olivia Gans and Mary Spaulding Balch assert, an embryo "has a beating heart [in] as early as 18 days, with tiny little fingers and toes. All her genetic definition of who she is for now and always—the color of her eyes, her hair, how tall she will grow to be—was present at the moment of fertilization. Therefore, in every abortion a helpless someone dies."

Many supporters of abortion rights concede that a fertilized human egg is a potential individual, but they insist that it is not yet a person. Although a zygote is alive and belongs to the species *homo sapiens*, they maintain, it is unable to live outside of the womb and should not be seen as an entity that is separate from the mother's body. As radio commentator Leonard Peikoff contends, "During the first trimester [the embryo] is a mass of relatively undifferentiated cells that exist as part of a woman's body. . . . It is not an independently existing, biologically formed organism, let alone a person." Moreover, Peikoff explains, since an embryo is not a person, it has no defendable right to life: "That which lives within the body of another can claim no right against its host. Rights belong only to individuals, . . . not to parts of an individual."

The question of when "personhood" begins is just one of the moral quandaries associated with the controversy over abortion. In the following chapter, theologians, opinion columnists, and activists consider whether abortion is ethical and consistent with the values of human rights.

> *"Direct abortion is* never *a morally tolerable option. It is* always *a grave act of violence against a woman and her unborn child."*

Abortion Is Immoral

Catholic Bishops of the United States

The following viewpoint is excerpted from a November 1998 statement drafted by the Catholic Bishops of the United States that addressed the American Catholic responsibility in opposing abortion in the political sphere. These bishops maintain that the most basic human right is the right to life. Since human life is sacred from conception until natural death, they contend, abortion is immoral. The bishops argue, furthermore, that the legalization of abortion in the United States has created a cultural environment in which other infractions against life—such as fetal experimentation, infanticide, and euthanasia—have become more acceptable. Americans must return to a morality that upholds the sanctity of all human life, they conclude.

As you read, consider the following questions:
1. In the authors' opinion, what are the "seeds of failure" that threaten American culture?
2. In what way does the Declaration of Independence advocate for the right to life, according to the bishops?
3. What role should women take in advancing the sanctity of life, in the authors' view?

Reprinted, with permission, from *Living the Gospel of Life: A Challenge to American Catholics*, a statement by the Catholic Bishops of the United States, November 1998. Copyright © 1998 United States Catholic Conference, Inc.

Now the word of the Lord came to me saying:
Before I formed you in the womb I knew you, before
you were born, I consecrated you; a prophet to the
nations I appointed you.

Jeremiah 1:5

When Henry Luce published his appeal for an "American century" in 1941, he could not have known how the coming reality would dwarf his dream. Luce hoped that the "engineers, scientists, doctors . . . builders of roads [and] teachers" of the United States would spread across the globe to promote economic success and American ideals: "a love of freedom, a feeling for the quality of opportunity, a tradition of self-reliance and independence and also cooperation."[1] Exactly this, and much more, has happened in the decades since. U.S. economic success has reshaped the world. But the nobility of the American experiment flows from its founding principles, not from its commercial power. In the twentieth century alone, hundreds of thousands of Americans have died defending those principles. Hundreds of thousands more have lived lives of service to those principles—both at home and on other continents—teaching, advising and providing humanitarian assistance to people in need. As Pope John Paul has observed, "At the center of the moral vision of [the American] founding documents is the recognition of the rights of the human person. . . ." The greatness of the United States lies "especially [in its] respect for the dignity and sanctity of human life in all conditions and at all stages of development."[2]

This nobility of the American spirit endures today in those who struggle for social justice and equal opportunity for the disadvantaged. The United States has thrived because, at its best, it embodies a commitment to human freedom, human rights and human dignity. This is why the Holy Father tells us: ". . . [As] Americans, you are rightly proud of your country's great achievements."[3]

But success often bears the seeds of failure. U.S. economic and military power has sometimes led to grave injustices abroad. At home, it has fueled self-absorption, indifference and consumerist excess. Overconfidence in our power, made even more pronounced by advances in science and technology, has created the illusion of a life without natural boundaries and actions without consequences. The standards of the marketplace, instead of being guided by sound morality, threaten to displace it. We are now witnessing the gradual restructuring of American culture according to ideals of utility, productivity and cost-effectiveness. It is a culture where moral questions are submerged by a river of goods and services and where the misuse of marketing and public relations subverts public life.

The losers in this ethical sea change will be those who are elderly, poor, disabled and politically marginalized. None of these pass the utility test; and yet, they at least have a presence. They at least have the possibility of organizing to be heard. *Those who are unborn, infirm and terminally ill have no such advantage.* They have no "utility," and worse, they have no voice. As we tinker with the beginning, the end and even the intimate cell structure of life, we tinker with our own identity as a free nation dedicated to the dignity of the human person. . . .

The nature and urgency of this threat should not be misunderstood. [The pope states that] respect for the dignity of the human person demands a commitment to human rights across a broad spectrum: "Both as Americans and as followers of Christ, American Catholics must be committed to the defense of life in all its stages and in every condition."[4] The culture of death extends beyond our shores: famine and starvation, denial of health care and development around the world, the deadly violence of armed conflict and the scandalous arms trade that spawns such conflict. Our nation is witness to domestic violence, the spread of drugs, sexual activity which poses a threat to lives, and a reckless tampering with the world's ecological balance. Respect for human life calls us to defend life from these and other threats. It calls us as well to enhance the conditions for human living by helping to provide food, shelter and meaningful employment, beginning with those who are most in need. We live the Gospel of Life when we live in solidarity with the poor of the world, standing up for their lives and dignity. Yet abortion and euthanasia have become preeminent threats to human dignity because they directly attack life itself, the most fundamental human good and the condition for all others. They are committed against those who are weakest and most defenseless, those who are genuinely "the poorest of the poor." They are endorsed increasingly without the veil of euphemism, as supporters of abortion and euthanasia freely concede these are killing even as they promote them. Sadly, they are practiced in those communities which ordinarily provide a safe haven for the weak—the family and the healing professions. Such direct attacks on human life, once crimes, are today legitimized by governments sworn to protect the weak and marginalized.

It needn't be so. God, the Father of all nations, has blessed the American people with a tremendous reservoir of goodness. He has also graced our founders with the wisdom to establish political structures enabling all citizens to participate in promoting the inalienable rights of all. As Americans, as Catholics and as pastors of our people, we write therefore today *to call our fellow citizens back to our country's founding principles*, and most especially *to renew our national respect for the rights of those who are unborn, weak, disabled and terminally ill*. Real freedom rests on the inviolability of every person as a child of God. The inherent value of human life, at every stage and in every circumstance, is not a sectarian issue any more than the Declaration of Independence is a sectarian creed. . . .

Nations are not machines or equations. They are like ecosystems. A people's habits, beliefs, values and institutions intertwine like a root system. Poisoning one part will eventually poison it all. As a result, bad laws and bad court decisions produce degraded political thought and behavior, and vice versa. So it is with the legacy of *Roe vs. Wade*. *Roe* effectively legalized abortion throughout pregnancy for virtually any reason, or none at all. It is responsible for the grief of millions of women and men, and the killing of millions of unborn children in the past quarter century. Yet the weaknesses of the Supreme Court's 1973 reasoning are well known. They were acknowledged by the Supreme Court itself in the subsequent 1992 *Casey vs. Planned Parenthood* decision, which could find no better reason to uphold *Roe* than the habits Roe itself created by surviving for 20 years.[5] The feebleness and confusion of the *Casey* decision flow directly out of *Roe*'s own confusion. They are part of the same root system. Taking a distorted "right to privacy" to new heights, and developing a new moral calculus to justify it, *Roe* has spread through the American political ecology with toxic results.

Roe effectively *rendered the definition of human personhood flexible and negotiable*. It also implicitly excluded unborn children from human status. In doing so, *Roe* helped create an environment in which infanticide—a predictable next step along the continuum of killing—is now open to serious examination. Thanks ultimately to *Roe*, some today speculate publicly and sympathetically why a number of young American women kill their newborn babies or leave them to die. Even the word "infanticide" is being replaced by new and less emotionally charged words like "neonaticide" (killing a newborn on the day of his or her birth) and "filicide" (killing the baby at some later point). Revising the name given to the killing *reduces its perceived gravity*. This is the ecology of law, moral reasoning and language in action. Bad law and defective moral reasoning produce the evasive language to justify evil. Nothing else can explain the verbal and ethical gymnastics required by elected officials to justify their support for partial-birth abortion, a procedure in which infants are brutally killed during the process of delivery. The same sanitized marketing is now deployed on behalf of physician-assisted suicide, fetal experimentation and human cloning. Each reduces the human person to a problem or an object. Each can trace its lineage in no small part to *Roe*. . . .

We believe that universal understandings of freedom and truth are "written on the human heart." America's founders also believed this to be true. In 1776 John Dickinson, one of the framers of our Constitution, affirmed: "Our liberties do not come from charters; for these are only the declaration of pre-existing rights. They do not depend on parchments or seals, but come from the king of kings and the Lord of all the earth."[6] The words of the Declaration of Independence speak of the "Laws of Nature and of Nature's God," and proceed to make the historic assertion: "We hold these truths to be self-evident, that all men are created equal, that they are endowed by their Creator with certain unalienable

Rights, that among these are Life, Liberty and the pursuit of Happiness. . . ." Today, more than two centuries of the American experiment have passed. We tend to take these words for granted. But for the founders, writing on the brink of armed revolution, these phrases were invested not just with their philosophy but with their lives. This is why they closed with a "firm reliance on the protection of divine Providence." The words of the Declaration of Independence illuminate the founding principles of the American Republic, principles explicitly grounded in unchanging truths about the human person.

Human Life Is Sacred

Human life is sacred and inviolable at every moment of existence, including the initial phase which precedes birth. All human beings, from their mothers' womb, belong to God who searches them and knows them, who forms them and knits them together with his own hands, who gazes on them when they are tiny shapeless embryos and already sees in them the adults of tomorrow whose days are numbered and whose vocation is even now written in the "book of life" [cf. Psalms 139:1, 13–16]. There too, when they are still in their mothers' womb—as many passages of the Bible bear witness—they are the personal objects of God's loving and fatherly providence.

John Paul II, *Origins*, April 6, 1995.

The principles of the Declaration were not fully reflected in the social or political structures of its own day. Then human slavery and other social injustices stood in tension to the high ideals the Founders articulated. Only after much time and effort have these contradictions been reduced. In a striking way, we see today a heightening of the tension between our nation's founding principles and political reality. We see this in diminishing respect for the inalienable right to life and in the elimination of legal protections for those who are most vulnerable. There can be no genuine justice in our society until the truths on which our nation was founded are more perfectly realized in our culture and law.

One of those truths is our own essential creatureliness. Virtual reality and genetic science may give us the illusion of power, but we are not gods. We are not our own, or anyone else's, creator. Nor, for our own safety, should we ever seek to be. Even parents, entrusted with a special guardianship over new life, do not "own" their children any more than one adult can own another. And therein lies our only security. *No one but the Creator is the sovereign of basic human rights—beginning with the right to life.* We are daughters and sons of the one God who, outside and above us all, grants us the freedom, dignity and rights of personhood which no one else can take away. Only in this context, the context of a Creator who authors our human dignity, do words like "truths" and "self-evident" find their ultimate meaning. Without the assumption that a Creator exists who has ordained certain irrevocable truths about the human person, no rights are "unalienable," and nothing about human dignity is axiomatic. . . .

Living the Gospel of Life: The Virtues We Need

Bringing a respect for human dignity to practical politics can be a daunting task. There is such a wide spectrum of issues involving the protection of human life and the promotion of human dignity. Good people frequently disagree on which problems to address, which policies to adopt and how best to apply them. But for citizens and elected officials alike, the basic principle is simple: *We must begin with a commitment never to intentionally kill, or collude in the killing, of any innocent human life, no matter how broken, unformed, disabled or desperate that life may seem.* In other words, the choice of certain ways of acting is *always and radically incompatible* with the love of God and the dignity of the human person created in His image. Direct abortion is *never* a morally tolerable option. It is *always* a grave act of violence against a woman and her unborn child. This is so even when a woman does not see the truth because of the pressures she may be subjected to, often by the child's father, her parents or friends. . . .

Adopting a consistent ethic of life, the Catholic Church promotes a broad spectrum of issues "seeking to protect human life and promote human dignity from the inception of life to its final moment."[7] Opposition to abortion and euthanasia does not excuse indifference to those who suffer from poverty, violence and injustice. Any politics of human life must work to resist the violence of war and the scandal of capital punishment. Any politics of human dignity must seriously address issues of racism, poverty, hunger, employment, education, housing, and health care. Therefore, Catholics should eagerly involve themselves as advocates for the weak and marginalized in all these areas. Catholic public officials are obliged to address each of these issues as they seek to build consistent policies which promote respect for the human person at all stages of life. *But being 'right' in such matters can never excuse a wrong choice regarding direct attacks on innocent human life.* Indeed, the failure to protect and defend life in its most vulnerable stages renders suspect any claims to the 'rightness' of positions in other matters affecting the poorest and least powerful of the human community. If we understand the human person as the "temple of the Holy Spirit"—the living house of God—then these latter issues fall logically into place as the crossbeams and walls of that house. *All direct attacks on innocent human life, such as abortion and euthanasia, strike at the house's foundation.* These directly and immediately violate the human person's most fundamental right—the right to life. Neglect of these issues is the equivalent of building our house on sand. Such attacks cannot help but lull the social conscience in ways ultimately destructive of other human rights. . . .

We urge parents to recall the words of the Second Vatican Council and our Holy Father in *On the Family* (*Familiaris Consortio*), that the family is "the first and vital cell of society." (42).[8] As the family goes, so goes our culture. Parents are the primary educators of their children, especially in the important areas of human sexuality and the transmission of human life. They shape society toward a respect for human life by first *being open to new life themselves*; then by forming their children—through personal example—with a reverence for the poor, the elderly and developing life in the womb. Families which live the Gospel of life are *important agents of evangelization through their witness*. But additionally, they should organize "to see that the laws and institutions of the state not only do not offend, but support and actively defend the rights and duties of the family," for the purpose of transforming society and advancing the sanctity of life. (44)

Women have a unique role in the transmission and nurturing of human life. They can best understand the bitter trauma of abortion and the hollowness and sterility at the heart of the vocabulary of "choice." Therefore, we ask women to assume a special role in promoting the Gospel of life with a new pro-life feminism. Women are uniquely qualified to counsel and support other women facing unexpected pregnancies, and they have been in the vanguard of establishing and staffing the more than 3000 pregnancy aid centers in the United States. They, in a way more fruitful than any others, can help elected officials to understand that any political agenda which hopes to uphold equal rights for all, must affirm the equal rights of every child, born and unborn. They can remind us that our nation's declaration of God-given rights, coupled with the command "Thou shalt not kill," are the starting points of true freedom. To choose any other path is to contradict our own identity as a nation dedicated to "life, liberty and the pursuit of happiness.". . .

As we . . . approach a new era for our own nation and the world, we believe that the purpose of the United States remains hopeful and worthy. In the words of Robert Frost, our vocation is to take *"the road less traveled," the road of human freedom rooted in law; law which is rooted, in turn, in the truth about the sanctity of the human person.* But the future of a nation is decided by every new generation. Freedom always implies the ability to choose between two roads: one which leads to life; the other, death (Dt 30:19). *It is now our turn to choose.* We appeal to all people of the United States, especially those in authority, and among them most especially Catholics, to understand this critical choice before us. We urge all persons of good will to work earnestly to bring about the cultural transformation we need, a true renewal in our public life and institutions based on the sanctity of all human life. And finally, as God entrusted His Son to Mary nearly 2,000 years ago for the redemption of the world, we close this letter today by entrusting to Mary all our people's efforts to witness the Gospel of life effectively in the public square.

> Mary, patroness of America, renew in us a love for the beauty and sanctity of the human person from conception to natural death; and as your Son gave His life for us, help us to live

our lives serving others. Mother of the Church, Mother of our Savior, open our hearts to the Gospel of life, protect our nation, and make us witnesses to the truth.

Notes

1. Henry Luce, "The American Century," *Life* (February 17, 1941).

2. Pope John Paul II, Departure from Baltimore/Washington International Airport, Departure Remarks, October 8, 1995; 25 *Origins*, p. 318 (October 19, 1995).

3. Pope John Paul II, Homily in Giants Stadium, October 5, 1995; 25 *Origins*, p. 305 (October 19, 1995).

4. Pope John Paul II, Homily in Giants Stadium, October 5, 1995; 25 *Origins*, p. 303 (October 19, 1995).

5. In *Planned Parenthood v. Casey*, 505 U.S. 833 (1992), the Supreme Court upheld most of the challenged provisions of a Pennsylvania law regulating abortion. The Court declined, however, to overturn what it called the "central holding" of *Roe v. Wade* and said: "[F]or two decades of economic and social developments, people have organized intimate relationships and made choices that define their views of themselves and their places in society, in reliance on the availability of abortion in the event that contraception should fail." 505 U.S. at 856.

6. Pope John Paul II, Remarks on accepting the credentials of the U.S. Ambassador to the Holy See, December 16, 1997; 27 *Origins*, p. 488 (January 8, 1998) [citing C. Herman Pritchett, *The American Constitution* (McGraw-Hill 1977), p. 2].

7. Administrative Board, United States Catholic Conference, *Political Responsibility: Proclaiming the Gospel of Life, Protecting the Least Among Us, and Pursuing the Common Good* (1995), p. 12.

8. Cf. also *Decree on the Apostolate of Lay People (Apostolicam Actuositatem)*, 11.

"Nowhere in the Scriptures is there any reference to sacredness or sanctity or respect for fetal life."

Abortion Is Not Immoral

John M. Swomley

In the following viewpoint, John M. Swomley provides a rebuttal to a November 1998 Catholic bishops' statement, which counseled Americans to protect human life from conception to death. Swomley contends that the bishops' argument cites the Bible out of context and imposes an anti-abortion agenda on the Scriptures. The Bible actually contains no statements against abortion, he explains; in addition, a fetus is scientifically defined as a person when brain activity begins—about twenty-eight weeks after implantation—not at conception. Abortion may be necessary when a woman's life, health, or family is endangered by her pregnancy, Swomley asserts. Ultimately, he concludes, women should have the right to control their destinies. Swomley is a professor emeritus of social ethics at St. Paul School of Theology in Kansas City, Missouri.

As you read, consider the following questions:
1. Under what circumstances did colonial America permit abortion, according to Swomley?
2. In the author's opinion, what is problematic about the phrase "sanctity of life"?
3. How does Swomley define "fetal idolatry"?

Excerpted from "Analysis of the Roman Catholic Bishops' November 1998 Political Pastoral Statement 'Living the Gospel of Life: A Challenge to American Catholics,'" by John M. Swomley, *The Human Quest*, March/April 1999. Reprinted with permission.

The 27-page Catholic bishops' statement, "Living the Gospel of Life," begins with a statement of the pope and also the bishops as to why American political, economic and cultural power, which have "reshaped the world" should now accept Vatican morality and lead the world in that direction.

This document is factually incorrect at essential main points.

Distortion of History

The bishops try to appeal to American Catholics' pride in our country's history: "As Americans, as Catholics, and as pastors of our people, we . . . call our fellow citizens back to our country's founding principles, and most especially to renew our national respect for the rights of the unborn."

Fact: In colonial America and even after the Constitution was adopted, English Common Law was in effect. It permitted abortion before fetal movement or "quickening," which was generally detectable after about the 16th week of pregnancy. The Articles of Confederation, the Declaration of Independence and the Constitution have no mention of any rights for the unborn. There were no laws with respect to abortion in the U.S. prior to 1821 in Connecticut, 1827 in Illinois, and 1830 in New York.

A New Jersey case, *State vs. Murphy*, explained the purpose of the state statute of 1849. That decision said: "The design of the statute was not to prevent the procuring of abortions, so much as to guard the health and life of the mother against the consequences of such attempts. . . . It is immaterial whether the fetus is destroyed or whether it has quickened or not. . . ."

America's founding principles made no reference to rights of the unborn, as the bishops assert. It is dishonest to attempt to make the phrase in the Declaration of Independence about the "laws of Nature and of Nature's God" mean what the pope means by natural law. It is also dishonest to assert that "all men are created equal" refers to male and female fetuses, when it didn't even refer to slaves and women as having equal rights.

When the bishops also quote the phrase, "certain inalienable rights. . . . Among these are life, liberty and the pursuit of happiness," they emphasize life for a fetus instead of the life and liberty of a woman to choose whether or not to continue a problem pregnancy. The authors of the founding documents of the United States did not even consider these words as dealing with fetal life or abortion.

A Sectarian Statement

The bishops state: "The inherent value of human life is not a sectarian issue any more than the Declaration of Independence is a sectarian creed."

Fact: The word "sectarian" refers to issues or actions that are fostered by church dogma on which some or all other religious groups differ. The Declaration of Independence is not a creed, but a political manifesto which referred to men (not the unborn) as having "inalienable" rights. The bishops' statement *is* sectarian in its reference to embryonic and fetal life and is not concerned with the life or health of a woman but only with the contents of her womb.

The bishops' statement, which is intended to implement papal doctrine, is also sectarian precisely because it is a statement by the Catholic hierarchy, not accepted by many Catholics and most Jews, Protestants and Humanists. The bishops also, again and again, direct it to Catholic members, Catholic politicians and voters, and invoke quotations from the pope. The statement also ends with a prayer to Mary, mother of the church.

Biblical Distortion

The bishops' statement quotes Jeremiah 1:5 at the very beginning. Jeremiah says, "Now the word of the Lord came to me saying, 'Before I formed you in the womb I knew you: before you were born, I consecrated you; a prophet to the nations I appointed you.'"

Fact: Jeremiah is making a claim about his credentials and authority to preach. He did not make a comment about whether God creates every conceptus, or has known us before we were conceived and, therefore, wills that every conceptus come to term.

Until the present abortion controversy, this passage was identified as a vocational call, having nothing to do with abortion. Later, in Jeremiah 15:10 and 20:17, Jeremiah regrets that he was born and that he did not die in his mother's womb.

The bishops should know that an important principle in understanding Scripture is exegesis: what does the writer say in context? Exegesis does not permit us to take a passage that deals with a specific situation or issue and turn it into a partisan or modern abortion text.

Jesus and Sanctity of Life

The bishops say Catholics should "recover their identity as followers of Jesus Christ and be leaders in the renewal of America's respect for the sanctity of life."

Fact: Jesus never mentioned abortion or sanctity of life. Nowhere in the Scriptures is there any reference to sacredness or sanctity or respect for fetal life. The only reference that comes close to this is Luke 2:23: "Every male that opens the womb shall be called holy to the Lord." It is characteristic of both Jewish and Christian Scripture that one must be born to be respected or to participate in the holy.

Just what does "sanctity of life" mean? Does it mean that all life must be treated with reverence and respect? Does it mean that embryonic life is more sacred than the life or health of the woman? The problem which cardinals and bishops do not face is that of conflict between existing persons and potential persons. They don't face the question of whether there should be a bias in favor of the woman. They promote a bias in favor of an embryo or fetus that may miscarry up to 50 percent of the time. What about a woman with diabetes, epilepsy or some other disease that would jeopardize her life if she continued a pregnancy to term? Is her life sacred?

Catholic ethicist Daniel Callahan refers to "the case of a mother with too many children and too few material, familial, social or psychological resources to care for them" and concludes that "the full human meaning of the act of abortion is preservation of the existing children."

Apparently the bishops define "sanctity of life" as fetal life that is inviolable. This means that all other human rights are ignored by the need to preserve embryonic and fetal life. In other words, Vatican legalism does not permit an examination of the context in which pregnant women find themselves. For example, a mother with three or four children whose husband with a recent heart attack can no longer support the family and she has to do so. Or a woman with one disabled child who is told she is bearing another deformed fetus that will require full-time care. The bishops do not take responsibility for such problems. They won't even take such problem children into their parochial schools without complete government funding.

Emergency Abortions

When the bishops launched the campaign against "partial birth abortions," they did not take into account that such late-term emergency abortions were performed on women who wanted a baby, many of them Catholics opposed to abortion. There are numerous case studies of such abortions, medically known as dilation and extraction (D & X), but one must suffice here:

Coreen Costello from Agoura, California, in April 1995 was pregnant with her third child. She and her husband found out that a lethal neuromuscular disease had left their much-wanted daughter unable to survive. Its body had stiffened and was frozen, wedged in a transverse position. In addition, amniotic fluid had puddled and built up to dangerous levels in Coreen's uterus. Devout Christians and opposed to abortion, the Costellos agonized for over two weeks about their decision and baptized the fetus in utero. Finally, Coreen's increasing health problems forced them to accept the advice of numerous medical experts that the intact dilation and extraction (D & X) was, indeed, the best option for Coreen's own health, and the abortion was performed. Later, in June 1996, Coreen gave birth to a healthy son.

Again and again, the bishops try to associate their anti-abortion position with the Gospel. Although abortion was widely practiced in the ancient world, there is not one reference against abortion in the entire New Testament. Even in the Hebrew Scripture or Old Testament, the only reference to individual abortion is in Numbers 5, where God commanded an abortion with respect to an unfaithful wife. Elsewhere God is quoted as having ordered many hundreds of abortions. In

Isaiah 13 and Hosea 13 there are references to "ripping up women with child" and destroying "the fruit of the womb."

When Does Human Life Begin?

The bishops state: "The point when human life begins is not a religious belief but a scientific fact."

Fact: Human life exists in the sperm and ovum. The real question is when does human life become a human being or person. It is misleading to speak of "a moment of conception" when sperm meets egg following sexual intercourse. Conception is not complete until the fertilized egg is implanted in the uterus, which generally occurs about 10 days to two weeks after ovulation. Up to 50 percent of fertilized eggs do not implant, and in those cases it is not possible to speak of conception. Except in cases of in vitro fertilization, it is impossible to know that fertilization has taken place until implantation occurs.

"Your life is in danger? So what?! We're only concerned with the sanctity of life!"

Beattie. Reprinted by permission of Copley News Service.

Charles Gardner, who did his doctoral research on the genetic control of brain development at the University of Michigan Medical School's Department of Anatomy and Cell Biology, says, "The 'biological' argument that a human being is created at fertilization . . . comes as a surprise to most embryologists . . . for it contradicts all that they have learned in the past few decades."

Gardner notes that "in humans when two sibling embryos combine into one, the resultant person may be completely normal. If the two original embryos were determined to become particular individuals, such a thing could not happen. The embryos would recognize themselves to be different . . . and would not unite. But here the cells seem unaware of any distinction between themselves. . . . The only explanation is that the individual is not fixed or determined at this stage."

Gardner also notes, "The fertilized egg is clearly not a prepackaged human being. . . . Our genes give us a propensity for certain characteristics. So how can an embryo be a human being? . . . The information to make an eye or a finger does not exist in the fertilized egg. It exists in the positions and interactions of cells and molecules that will be formed at a later date."

Such research and discoveries lead to the conclusion that it is a developmental process taking about nine months that produces a human being or person. Therefore, the Vatican idea that a human exists at conception is a theological statement rather than a medical or scientific fact.

Gardner concludes that "fertilization, the injection of sperm DNA into the egg, is just one of the many small steps toward full human potential. It seems arbitrary to invest this biological event with any special moral significance. . . . It would be a great tragedy if, in ignorance of the process that is the embryo, state legislators pass laws restricting the individual freedom of choice and press them upon the people. The embryo is not a child. It is not a baby. It is not yet a human being."

The Human Person

The bishops attack abortion as a "violation of the human person's most fundamental right—the right to life." In fact, the bishops use "human life" and "person's life" interchangeably, even though the Vatican has not proclaimed an embryo or conceptus as a person. When is there a person? The brain is the crucial element of personhood, and a statement by 167 scientists indicates that "at about 28 weeks of gestation, brain development is marked by the sudden emergence of dendritic spines in the neocortex. Dendritic spines are essential components in the brain's cellular circuitry.

Michael V.L. Bennett, chair of the Department of Neuroscience, Albert Einstein College of Medicine, wrote that "personhood goes with the brain and does not reside within the recipient body. . . . There is none, not heart, kidney, lung or spleen that we cannot transplant, do without, or replace artificially. The brain is the essence of our existence. It cannot be transplanted."

The Right to Life

The bishops speak about the "most fundamental right—the right to life." In discussing this claim we must distinguish between a virtue, that is, doing something that may be desirable, and a right. If I am walking along a river and someone who can't swim falls or jumps in, she/he cannot claim that I must jump in to rescue her because she has a right to life. The mere fact that I ought to rescue another does not give that person or society a right against me.

The common law rule is that we have no duty to save the life of another person unless we voluntarily undertake such an obligation, as a lifeguard does in contracting to save lives at a swimming pool. No woman should be required to give up her life or health or family security to save the life of a fetus that is threatening her well-being. At the very least she is entitled to self-defense. Moreover, the act of intercourse is not a contract for pregnancy. Even less should the act of rape be regarded as a guarantee, to a resulting fetus, of the right to life.

The bishops also appeal to the Sixth of the Ten Commandments: "Thou shalt not kill." This was and is not applicable to fetal life but refers to those who are human persons, as do all the other commandments. However, in the same Mosaic law there is a listing of those to be put to death, such as those who curse father or mother. In so doing the bishops show their lack of regard for biblical admonition and are special pleaders for a position not validated in the Bible.

Fetal Idolatry

The bishops refer to "idolatry of the self" or the placing of "my needs, my appetites, my choices to the exclusion of moral restraints." Actually, the bishops are engaging in fetal idolatry in absolutizing the sacredness of the fetus. Like an *Old Testament* idol, the fetus is something for which a sacrifice must be offered. Fetal idolatry denies a woman's right to control her body, her life, her destiny, which must be sacrificed to an embryo or fetus once she is pregnant.

Fetal idolatry is bolstered by two other idolatries. One is patriarchy and the second is religious hierarchy. Both are evident in the subordination of women to men, who have historically made political, economic and religious decisions for women. In this "sanctity" of fetal life, a male hierarchy is attempting to make a virtue out of women's subordination. For years the Republican Party platform echoed Vatican doctrine with this statement: "The unborn child has a fundamental right to life that cannot be infringed." This means, as does the bishops' statement, that men and fetuses have a fundamental right to life, but pregnant women do not.

"A death occurs every time an abortion is performed—the death of an unborn child."

Abortion Violates Human Rights

Carolyn C. Gargaro

Abortion is wrong because it entails the killing of innocent human life, maintains Carolyn C. Gargaro in the following viewpoint. Human life begins with the union of sperm and egg, she argues, because fertilization creates a unique individual with a complete genetic code. Furthermore, since an unborn child has a different genetic makeup from that of its mother, its life should be seen as something that is separate and distinct from the mother. All unborn children, therefore, are fully human and should have their fundamental right to life protected, the author asserts. Gargaro is a freelance writer and web page developer.

As you read, consider the following questions:

1. According to Gargaro, what are some of the legal rights that unborn children have?
2. What risks does abortion pose for women, according to the author?
3. In Gargaro's opinion, why should fetal viability *not* determine an unborn child's right to life?

Excerpted from "My Views as a Pro-Life Woman," by Carolyn C. Gargaro, February 5, 2000, found at www.gargaro.com/abortion.html. Reprinted with permission.

Today, more than twenty-seven years since the legalization of abortion, over 30 million legal abortions have taken place in the United States. To me, this is an issue which is more than a simple question of women controlling their own lives and bodies. It is a matter of life and death for an innocent human being.

Right away, some will say that abortion is not a matter of life and death, arguing that a fetus is not a "person", or a "human being". Yet, medical research proves that the fetus is a living organism from the moment of conception. Though it may be argued that this living organism is not a person, it seems that it can be nothing other than a human being. I realize that it may be difficult to think of a three-week old fetus as a human with rights. The way I think to best explain this is to start by going back to the sperm and the egg.

Life Begins at Fertilization

A sperm has 23 chromosomes, and no matter what, even though it is alive and can fertilize an egg, it can never make another sperm. An egg also has 23 chromosomes and it can never make another egg. So we have eggs and sperm that cannot reproduce. A solitary egg or a solitary sperm does not have the complete genetic code for a separate human being. The ovum and the sperm are each a product of another's body: unlike the fertilized egg, neither is an independent entity. Neither one is complete. Like cells in someone's hair or fingernails, an egg or sperm does not have the capacity to become other than what it already is. Both are essentially dead-ends, destined to remain what they are until they die in a matter of days. This negates one common argument—that the unborn isn't human, or else every time a man ejaculated, or a woman menstruated, an "unborn" dies. Obviously this is ridiculous—a sperm without an egg and an egg without a sperm does not constitute human life.

Once there is the union of a sperm and egg, the 23 chromosomes are brought together in one cell with 46 chromosomes. Once there are 46 chromosomes, that one cell has all of the DNA, the whole genetic code for a genetically distinct human life. It isn't a "potential" human life, or some "other" type of life because something non-human does not magically become human by getting older and bigger—whatever is human must be human from the beginning. Everything that constitutes a human being is present from that moment forward—the only thing added from that point on is nutrition so the unborn can grow. This new life is not a sperm or an egg, or even a simple combination of both. It is independent with a life of its own, and the development is actually self-directed. A sperm can't do that—neither can an egg. They do not "develop".

The baby's blood supply is also completely separate from the mother's. If they are not separate bodies, how could a mother and child have different blood types? If a child's and mother's blood mix, it can be fatal for the child if the Rh factors are different. There is a shot to prevent this, but if there is not, and the blood of different Rh factors mix, the baby can die. Now, I cannot think of any doctor that would kill a newborn baby the moment that it was born. My question is, now, can that baby be killed a minute before it is born, or a minute before that, or a minute before that? You see what I'm getting at. At what minute can one consider life to be worthless and at the next minute that life to be precious?

Even most medical texts and pro-choice doctors agree with geneticist Ashley Montagu, who has written: "The basic fact is simple: life begins not at birth, but at conception." The beginning of human life is not a religious, moral, or philosophical issue; it is a scientific and biological one. From the time those 23 chromosomes become 46 onward, the unborn is a living, developing individual with a unique genetic makeup.

Medical Ethics?

What surprised me most was statements from abortionists themselves who seemed to know that they were destroying life, a human life. For instance:

Neville Sender, M.D., who runs an abortion clinic, Metropolitan Medical Service, in Milwaukee, Wisconsin: "We know it is killing, but the states permit killing under certain circumstances."

Warren Hern, M.D., of the Boulder Abortion Clinic in Boulder, Colorado: "There is no possibility of denial of an act of destruction by the operator. It is before one's eyes. The sensations of dismemberment flow through the forceps like an electric current."

Abortionist at a New York City hospital, as quoted by psychologist Magda Denes in her book, *In Necessity and Sorrow*: "Even now I feel a little peculiar about it, because as a physician I'm trained to conserve life and here I am destroying life."

Ron Fitzsimmons, executive director of the National Coalition of Abortion Providers: "Women enter abortion clinics to kill their fetuses. It is a form of killing. You're ending a life."

So much for medical ethics.

The Rights of the Unborn

I hope to have at least shown that the unborn is a human individual. It is also interesting that this individual, who can be denied life, has other rights. An unborn baby can be injured in an accident and at a later date, after being born, can sue the person who has injured him; a fetus can inherit an estate and take precedence over a person who is already born as soon as that fetus himself is born. In addition, the US Congress voted unanimously in 1974 to delay the capital punishment of pregnant women until after they have given birth.

The problem I have with abortion is: why should we deny this individual the right to live? At what point is the unborn worthy to live? I realize that there are other difficult questions regarding abortion, and I will address a few of them.

Some believe that even though there may be life, or potential life, or however one wants to refer to the fetus, that denying a woman the right to an abortion is denying her control of her body. Being a woman myself, I am obviously against people trying to control women or their bodies. But the fetus is a completely separate life from the woman. It has a completely different blood type and genetic code; it is not just part of the mother's body. It is temporarily residing there, and birth is just the change of residence from an already living, active person. Just because the unborn is dependent on the mother for nine months, does that give anyone the right to choose to end its life? Being dependent on others should not deprive a helpless human being the fundamental right to live, as we do not base humanness on whether another person is around to take care of that life. Trying to justify abortion by arguing that the unborn does not have this right is a form of discrimination based on age and the fact that they cannot speak for themselves.

What About "Unwanted" Children?

There is also an issue about child abuse, that unwanted children will be unloved and abused. There are two tough questions here. First, what does "unwanted" mean? If the mother does not want the child, there are thousands of childless couples who certainly would want that child. Also, someone's right to live should not be based on how much one individual wants them. Do we dispose of born children who are abandoned and obviously not wanted?

The Violent Killing of a Baby

Now, I want to be the first to admit that not everyone sees abortion as the ending of a life. There are probably some people who still see a baby in the womb as unfeeling tissue, like a mole or subcutaneous fat. They see the baby in the sonogram looking like a baby and they don't believe it's a baby. They see the baby reacting to a needle and moving away from it and they don't think it's a life. They know that a baby in the womb relaxes when she or he hears soothing music and they don't think there's a baby there. There are people who know that babies look just like postpartum babies very soon after conception, when they are still in the womb, and have a strong sense of pain, but those people can still call an abortion something other than the violent killing of a baby. None so blind as those who will not see, goes the adage.

Benjamin J. Stein, *American Spectator*, May 1998.

There are also countless programs across the country that can provide counseling, housing, medical care, job training and other services for anyone with an unplanned pregnancy who would want to keep their child. Many loving couples are also seeking to adopt children—in fact, there are many more parents waiting to adopt children of all types—white, black, handicapped or not—than there are available children.

Secondly, there is no correlation between unplanned

pregnancies and the subsequent abuse of the children—in fact, it is most often the *wanted* children who are abused. For instance, a study of 674 battered children in California found that 91% of the children were wanted, compared to 63% for the control groups nationally. I have not yet seen a study (and I have read a large amount of pro-choice material) that correlates the two.

Child abuse has also increased by 500% since abortion was legalized in 1973. . . .

The Dangers of Abortion

I would also like to address the potential problem of women seeking "back-alley," or illegal abortions if abortion is not kept legal. What is interesting about this argument is that *Roe v. Wade* basically made people who were previously considered illegal abortionists, now legal abortionists! As quoted in *Roe v. Wade*: "The state is constitutionally barred, however, from requiring review of the abortion decision by a hospital committee or concurrence in the decision by two physicians other than the attending physician. The Constitution also prohibits a state from requiring that the abortion be in a hospital licensed by the Joint Committee on Accreditation of Hospitals or indeed that it be a hospital at all." By virtually eliminating state regulation of abortions, the Court simply let illegal "back-alley" abortionists to go legal, with their procedures unchanged.

It should also be remembered that a death occurs every time an abortion is performed—the death of an unborn child. Women have control over choosing an illegal abortion that they know could be harmful. The unborn has absolutely no control when the mother chooses to abort. In addition, abortion is a surgical procedure, and even though it is legal, it still puts many women at risk. Many women suffer post-abortion complications, such as severe muscle damage and damage to the uterine wall, which can lead to scarring, future miscarriages, ectopic pregnancies, and other future medical problems. In addition, induced abortion approximately triples the risk of suicide; women who carry full-term have about 1/2 the risk of suicide as the general female population.

41

Viability Does Not Determine Personhood

Many people who I've talked to say, "Well, abortion is acceptable because it's done before the fetus is viable." First, viability is not something which should be used to determine whether someone is "human enough" to have the right to live, since viability is based on medical science. Medical science does not determine when someone becomes human. In 1990, a 25-week-old fetus could not survive outside the womb. Now it can. Maybe in ten years, a 15-week-old fetus will be able to be sustained outside the womb. Does this mean that the fetus, in 1999, is not human, but a fetus of the same age in 2007 is somehow more human? The point of viability constantly changes because it is based on medical technology, not the fetus itself. What if one hospital had the technology to keep a 20-week-old fetus alive but another hospital only had the technology to keep a 28-week-old fetus alive? Is the fetus "human" and worthy of life in one hospital but not in another?

Secondly, abortions *are* done after viability because abortion is basically legal the full nine months. As defined by the Supreme Court, "viable" is "capable of meaningful life." According to *Roe v. Wade*, after viability has been reached, the life is not a person in the "whole sense", so that even after viability the fetus is not protected by the Fourteenth Amendment's guarantee that life shall not be taken without due process of the law. States may, but are not required to, prohibit post-viability abortions. Only twenty-one prohibit them now. Only 1% of abortions occur after 20 weeks, and about 4/100ths of one percent (300–600 abortions) take place after 26 weeks. "Viability" is usually considered to be about 24 weeks, so it is difficult to pinpoint exactly how many "post-viability" abortions occur.

However, "late-term" abortions are described as abortions occurring after the 16th week, according to the Alan Guttmacher Institute, a well-known pro-choice institute. Many people believe that late-term abortions are only done for extreme circumstances, as is the case with most post-viability abortions, but this is not the case. In one pro-choice study of women who had an abortion after the 16th week, 71% said they "did not recognize that she was pregnant or misjudged gestation," and 24% "took time to decide to have an abortion." Only 2% said "a fetal problem was diagnosed late in pregnancy," and the report did not indicate that any of the late abortions were performed because of maternal health problems. Look at a picture of a baby aborted in the fifth month of pregnancy, and then try and say abortion does not end a human life.

Most Americans Are Pro-Life

Despite the opinion that I have heard from many people, the majority of the American public is pro-life. In addition, pro-life people are not against sex or women's rights. Sure, there are some radicals, but there are radicals in every group. Some say that the pro-life side is run by men who want to control women. This is untrue, and I think the situation may be reversed. How many women have had an abortion because they have been pressured by a man—their father, boyfriend, or husband? And who primarily performs abortions? Male doctors. In essence, I feel that making abortion an acceptable, and even preferred option in some cases, is yet another way to control women. Think about it—get the woman to have an abortion, and the man doesn't have to be burdened with any responsibility. If men were the ones who had to go through abortions, I'm sure the medical community would be much more interested in developing foolproof birth control. . . .

The pro-life stand is not just an anti-abortion stand. It is one to try and prevent unwanted pregnancies, and to take care of the mother and child if one does occur. Pro-lifers will also counsel people after an abortion if they suffer physically or psychologically. Women, especially teenagers, are often totally distraught after an abortion and have no one to turn to because the clinic did not offer post-abortion counseling. These girls have turned to people from the pro-life community for help, and they have been helped, not yelled at or condemned. To be hateful or vindictive towards these women is not the point. Pro-lifers stand up for the sacredness of life, and speak mainly out of love—love for the babies that we will never see, for the frightened women who don't understand what they are going through. I always urge

people to remember also, that it is the abortion clinic workers, not pro-life volunteers, who are receiving a financial
gain in persuading women into the choice of whether or not
to have an abortion.

What I also find interesting is that pro-lifers are always
asked the question, "If you're so compassionate, why don't
you take care of all the 'unwanted' children?" Using that
logic, if pro-lifers believe that abortion is wrong and thus
should pay for every "unwanted" child, then the pro-
choicers, who believe abortion is *not* wrong, should pay for
all women's abortions.

Funny, I've heard many stories of these "compassionate"
clinics turning women away if they didn't have enough
money. For instance, in March 1994, a single, unemployed
woman was turned away from a St. Petersburg abortion
clinic because she didn't have enough money.

There is no easy answer to this situation, and I do not
think unwanted pregnancies are something to be taken
lightly. However, I feel that the medical community should
emphasize finding safe and effective birth control that would
eliminate the need for abortion. That would be the easiest
solution, because even if *Roe v. Wade* is overturned, the debate will still rage on, and some abortions will still occur. But
before effective birth control is found, before society
changes its attitude toward pregnancy, and makes it more acceptable for women or young girls to be pregnant, the answer to this societal problem is not to kill the innocent.

"Abortion is an absolutely moral choice for any woman wishing to control her body."

Abortion Does Not Violate Human Rights

Brian Elroy McKinley

In the following viewpoint, Brian Elroy McKinley argues that although abortion destroys a potential human life, it is not murder. The embryo or fetus is not a separate human being because it is not able to survive outside the woman's body, he maintains. Only when a baby can live independently from its mother's body can it be granted full human rights. Until that point, McKinley claims, a fetus' rights should not supersede the rights of a woman to protect and control her body. McKinley is an Internet consultant who resides in Colorado.

As you read, consider the following questions:

1. What do an ameba and a human zygote have in common, according to McKinley?
2. In the author's opinion, what is the difference between a human and a person?
3. In the context of McKinley's argument, what is the difference between physical dependence and social dependence?

Reprinted, with permission, from "Why Abortion Is Moral," by Brian Elroy McKinley, 2000, found at http://elroy.net/ehr/abortionanswers.html.

All of the arguments against abortion boil down to six specific questions. The first five deal with the nature of the zygote-embryo-fetus growing inside a mother's womb. The last one looks at the morality of the practice. These questions are:

1. Is it alive?
2. Is it human?
3. Is it a person?
4. Is it physically independent?
5. Does it have human rights?
6. Is abortion murder?

Let's take a look at each of these questions. We'll show how anti-abortionists use seemingly logical answers to back up their cause, but then we'll show how their arguments actually support the fact that abortion is moral.

Is It Alive?

Yes. Pro-Choice supporters who claim it isn't do themselves and their cause a disservice. Of course it's alive. It's a biological mechanism that converts nutrients and oxygen into energy that causes its cells to divide, multiply, and grow. It's alive.

Anti-abortion activists often mistakenly use this fact to support their cause. "Life begins at conception" they claim. And they would be right. The genesis of a new human life begins when the egg with 23 chromosomes joins with a sperm with 23 chromosomes and creates a fertilized cell, called a zygote, with 46 chromosomes. The single-cell zygote contains all the DNA necessary to grow into an independent, conscious human being. It is a potential person.

But being alive does not give the zygote full human rights—including the right not to be aborted during its gestation.

A single-cell ameba also coverts nutrients and oxygen into biological energy that causes its cells to divide, multiply and grow. It also contains a full set of its own DNA. It shares everything in common with a human zygote except that it is not a potential person. Left to grow, it will always be an ameba—never a human person. It is just as alive as the zygote, but we would never defend its human rights based solely on that fact.

And neither can the anti-abortionist, which is why we must answer the following questions as well.

Is It Human?

Yes. Again, Pro-Choice defenders stick their feet in their mouths when they defend abortion by claiming the zygote-embryo-fetus isn't human. It is human. Its DNA is that of a human. Left to grow, it will become a full human person.

And again, anti-abortion activists often mistakenly use this fact to support their cause. They are fond of saying, "an acorn is an oak tree in an early stage of development; likewise, the zygote is a human being in an early stage of development." And they would be right. But having a full set of human DNA does not give the zygote full human rights—including the right not to be aborted during its gestation.

Don't believe me? Here, try this: reach up to your head, grab one strand of hair, and yank it out. Look at the base of the hair. That little blob of tissue at the end is a hair follicle. It also contains a full set of human DNA. Granted it's the same DNA pattern found in every other cell in your body, but in reality the uniqueness of the DNA is not what makes it a different person. Identical twins share the exact same DNA, and yet we don't say that one is less human than the other, nor are two twins the exact same person. It's not the configuration of the DNA that makes a zygote human; it's simply that it has human DNA. Your hair follicle shares everything in common with a human zygote except that it is a little bit bigger and it is not a potential person. (These days even that's not an absolute considering our new-found ability to clone humans from existing DNA, even the DNA from a hair follicle.)

Your hair follicle is just as human as the zygote, but we would never defend its human rights based solely on that fact.

And neither can the anti-abortionist, which is why the following two questions become critically important to the abortion debate.

Is It a Person?

No. It's merely a potential person.

Webster's Dictionary lists a person as "being an individual or existing as an indivisible whole; existing as a distinct entity." Anti-abortionists claim that each new fertilized zygote is already a new person because its DNA is uniquely different than anyone else's. In other words, if you're human, you must be a person.

Of course we've already seen that a simple hair follicle is just as human as a single-cell zygote, and, that unique DNA doesn't make the difference since two twins are not one person. It's quite obvious, then, that something else must occur to make one human being different from another. There must be something else that happens to change a DNA-patterned body into a distinct person. (Or in the case of twins, two identically DNA-patterned bodies into two distinct persons.)

There is, and most people inherently know it, but they have trouble verbalizing it for one very specific reason.

Consciousness

The defining mark between something that is human and someone who is a person is 'consciousness.' It is the self-aware quality of consciousness that makes us uniquely different from others. This self-awareness, this sentient consciousness is also what separates us from every other animal life form on the planet. We think about ourselves. We use language to describe ourselves. We are aware of ourselves as a part of the greater whole.

The problem is that consciousness normally doesn't occur until months, even years, after a baby is born. This creates a moral dilemma for the defender of abortion rights. Indeed, they inherently know what makes a human into a person, but they are also aware such individual personhood doesn't occur until well after birth. To use personhood as an argument for abortion rights, therefore, also leads to the argument that it should be okay to kill a 3-month-old baby since it hasn't obtained consciousness either.

Anti-abortionists use this perceived problem in an attempt to prove their point. In a debate, a Pro-Choice defender will rightly state that the difference between a fetus and a full-term human being is that the fetus isn't a person. The anti-abortion activist, being quite sly, will reply by asking his opponent to define what makes someone into a person. Suddenly the Pro-Choice defender is at a loss for words to describe what he or she knows innately. We know it because we lived it. We know we have no memory of self-awareness before our first birthday, or even before our second. But we also quickly become aware of the "problem" we create if we say a human doesn't become a person until well after its birth. And we end up saying nothing. The anti-abortionist then takes this inability to verbalize the nature of personhood as proof of their claim that a human is a person at conception.

But they are wrong. Their "logic" is greatly flawed. Just because someone is afraid to speak the truth doesn't make it any less true.

And in reality, the Pro-Choice defender's fear is unfounded. They are right, and they can state it without hesitation. A human indeed does not become a full person until consciousness. And consciousness doesn't occur until well after the birth of the child. But that does not automatically lend credence to the anti-abortionist's argument that it should, therefore, be acceptable to kill a three-month-old baby because it is not yet a person.

It is still a potential person. And after birth it is an independent potential person whose existence no longer poses a threat to the physical well-being of another. To understand this better, we need to look at the next question.

Is It Physically Independent?

No. It is absolutely dependent on another human being for its continued existence. Without the mother's life-giving nutrients and oxygen it would die. Throughout gestation the zygote-embryo-fetus and the mother's body are symbiotically linked, existing in the same physical space and sharing the same risks. What the mother does affects the fetus. And when things go wrong with the fetus, it affects the mother.

Anti-abortionists claim fetal dependence cannot be used as an issue in the abortion debate. They make the point that even after birth, and for years to come, a child is still dependent on its mother, its father, and those around it. And since no one would claim it's okay to kill a child because of its dependency on others, we can't, if we follow their logic, claim it's okay to abort a fetus because of its dependence.

What the anti-abortionist fails to do, however, is differentiate between physical dependence and social dependence. Physical dependence does not refer to meeting the physical needs of the child—such as in the anti-abortionist's argument above. That's social dependence; that's where the child depends on society—on other people—to feed it, clothe it, and love it. Physical dependence occurs when one life form depends solely on the physical body of another life form for its existence.

Physical dependence was cleverly illustrated back in 1971 by philosopher Judith Jarvis Thompson. She created a scenario in which a woman is kidnapped and wakes up to find she's been surgically attached to a world-famous violinist who, for nine months, needs her body to survive. After those nine months, the violinist can survive just fine on his own, but he must have this particular woman in order to survive until then.

Thompson then asks if the woman is morally obliged to stay connected to the violinist who is living off her body. It might be a very good thing if she did—the world could have the beauty that would come from such a violinist—but is she morally obliged to let another being use her body to survive?

This very situation is already conceded by anti-abortionists. They claim RU-486 should be illegal for a mother to take because it causes her uterus to flush its nutrient-rich lining, thus removing a zygote from its necessary support system and, therefore, ending its short existence as a life form. Thus the anti-abortionist's own rhetoric only proves the point of absolute physical dependence.

This question becomes even more profound when we consider a scenario where it's not an existing person who is living off the woman's body, but simply a potential person, or better yet, a single-cell zygote with human DNA that is no different than the DNA in a simple hair follicle.

A Physical Threat

To complicate it even further, we need to realize that physical dependence also means a physical threat to the life of the mother. The World Health Organization reports that nearly 670,000 women die from pregnancy-related complications each year (this number does not include abortions). That's 1,800 women per day. We also read that in developed countries, such as the United States and Canada, a woman is 13 times more likely to die bringing a pregnancy to term than by having an abortion.

Therefore, not only is pregnancy the prospect of having a potential person physically dependent on the body of one particular woman, it also includes the woman putting herself into a life-threatening situation for that potential person.

Embryos Are Not Independent

We must not confuse potentiality with actuality. An embryo is a potential human being. It can, granted the woman's choice, develop into an infant. But what it actually is during the first trimester is a mass of relatively undifferentiated cells that exist as a part of a woman's body. If we consider what it is rather than what it might become, we must acknowledge that the embryo under three months is something far more primitive than a frog or a fish. To compare it to an infant is ludicrous. . . .

That tiny growth, that mass of protoplasm, exists as a part of a woman's body. It is not an independently existing, biologically formed organism, let alone a person. That which lives within the body of another can claim no right against its host. Rights belong only to individuals, not to collectives or to parts of an individual.

Leonard Peikoff, online article, www.aynrand.org/medialink/profile.html, April 19, 1999.

Unlike social dependence, where the mother can choose to put her child up for adoption or make it a ward of the state or hire someone else to take care of it, during pregnancy the fetus is absolutely physically dependent on the body of one woman. Unlike social dependence, where a woman's physical life is not threatened by the existence of another person, during pregnancy, a woman places herself in the path of bodily harm for the benefit of a DNA life form that is only a potential person—even exposing herself to the threat of death.

This brings us to the next question: do the rights of a potential person supersede the rights of the mother to control her body and protect herself from potential life-threatening danger?

Does It Have Human Rights?

Yes and No.

A potential person must always be given full human rights unless its existence interferes with the rights of Life, Liberty, and the Pursuit of Happiness of an already existing conscious human being. Thus, a gestating fetus has no rights before birth and full rights after birth.

If a fetus comes to term and is born, it is because the mother chooses to forgo her own rights and her own bodily security in order to allow that future person to gestate inside her body. If the mother chooses to exercise control over her own body and to protect herself from the potential dangers of childbearing, then she has the full right to terminate the pregnancy.

Anti-abortion activists are fond of saying "The only difference between a fetus and a baby is a trip down the birth canal." This flippant phrase may make for catchy rhetoric, but it doesn't belay the fact that indeed "location" makes all the difference in the world.

It's actually quite simple. You cannot have two entities with equal rights occupying one body. One will automatically have veto power over the other—and thus they don't have equal rights. In the case of a pregnant woman, giving a "right to life" to the potential person in the womb automatically cancels out the mother's right to Life, Liberty, and the Pursuit of Happiness.

After birth, on the other hand, the potential person no longer occupies the same body as the mother, and thus, giving it full human rights causes no interference with another's right to control her body. Therefore, even though a full-term human baby may still not be a person, after birth it enjoys the full support of the law in protecting its rights. After birth its independence begs that it be protected as if it were equal to a fully-conscious human being. But before birth its lack of personhood and its threat to the woman in which it resides makes abortion a completely logical and moral choice.

Which brings us to our last question, which is the real crux of the issue. . . .

Is Abortion Murder?

No. Absolutely not.

It's not murder if it's not an independent person. One might argue, then, that it's not murder to end the life of any child before she reaches consciousness, but we don't know how long after birth personhood arrives for each new child, so it's completely logical to use their independence as the dividing line for when full rights are given to a new human being.

Using independence also solves the problem of dealing with premature babies. Although a preemie is obviously still only a potential person, by virtue of its independence from the mother, we give it the full rights of a conscious person. This saves us from setting some other arbitrary date of when we consider a new human being a full person. Older cultures used to set it at two years of age, or even older. Modern religious cultures want to set it at conception, which is simply wishful thinking on their part. As we've clearly demonstrated, a single-cell zygote is no more a person that a human hair follicle.

But that doesn't stop religious fanatics from dumping their judgements and their anger on top of women who choose to exercise the right to control their bodies. It's the ultimate irony that people who claim to represent a loving God resort to scare tactics and fear to support their mistaken beliefs.

It's even worse when you consider that most women who have an abortion have just made the most difficult decision of their life. No one thinks abortion is a wonderful thing. No one tries to get pregnant just so they can terminate it. Even though it's not murder, it still eliminates a potential person, a potential daughter, a potential son. It's hard enough as it is. Women certainly don't need others telling them it's a murder.

It's not. On the contrary, abortion is an absolutely moral choice for any woman wishing to control her body.

> "*Abortion is an evil whose magnitude is comparable to that of any 'crime against humanity.'*"

Abortion Is a Form of Genocide

Gregg Cunningham

Abortion is a form of genocide, argues Gregg Cunningham in the following viewpoint. Since 1973, more than 38 million unborn children have been systematically aborted in the United States—an occurrence that Cunningham maintains is a veritable modern-day holocaust. Moreover, today's justifications for abortion—such as the claim that fetuses are not persons or will place undue burdens on society—echo historical justifications for American slavery, racist lynchings, and the Jewish holocaust, the author contends. Cunningham is the director of the Los Angeles–based Center for Bio-Ethical Reform, an anti-abortion advocacy organization.

As you read, consider the following questions:
1. In what way does the Planned Parenthood motto "every child a wanted child" reveal a hatred of the unborn, according to Cunningham?
2. How does the definition of personhood in *Roe v. Wade* dehumanize unborn children, according to the author?
3. In Cunningham's opinion, what is wrong with the arguments of those who claim that they are personally opposed to abortion but support a woman's right to choose?

As part of its Genocide Awareness Project, The Center for Bio-Ethical Reform exhibits large photo murals comparing aborted babies with Jewish Holocaust victims, African Americans killed in racist lynchings, Native Americans exterminated by the US Army, etc. Our purpose is to illuminate the conceptual similarities which exist between abortion and more widely recognized forms of genocide. This is important because perpetrators of genocide always call it something else and the word "abortion" has, therefore, lost most of its meaning.

Visual depictions of abortion are indispensable to the restoration of that meaning because abortion represents an evil so inexpressible that words fail us when we attempt to describe its horror. Abortion will continue to be trivialized as "the lesser of two evils," or perhaps even "a necessary evil," as long as it is allowed to remain an invisible abstraction. Pictures make it impossible for anyone with a shred of intellectual honesty to maintain the pretense that "it's not a baby" and "abortion is not an act of violence." Pictures also make clear to people of conscience the fact that abortion is an evil whose magnitude is comparable to that of any "crime against humanity." Educators properly use shocking imagery to teach about genocide and we insist on the right to do the same.

We call this endeavor the Genocide Awareness Project (GAP) because *Webster's New World Encyclopedia* defines "genocide" as "The deliberate and systematic destruction of a national, racial, religious, political, cultural, ethnic, or other group defined by the exterminators as undesirable." That definition readily applies to abortion. The "national group" is American "unwanted" unborn children and they are now being destroyed at the rate of nearly 1 out of every 3 conceived. They are being terminated in an elaborate network of killing centers.

Is Abortion "Systematic"?

U.S. News & World Report, December 7, 1998, in an article entitled "Abortion: the untold story," quotes the Alan Guttmacher Institute as follows: "By 1992 . . . there were 2,400 abortion facilities . . ." in the U.S. The story adds that

". . . 70 percent of women of childbearing age lived in counties with abortion facilities . . ." and ". . . only 8 percent of the women who got abortions in 1992 . . . drove more than 100 miles . . ." to terminate their pregnancies. The article concludes with the admission that ". . . abortion-rights advocates acknowledge they don't personally know of women who wanted . . . an abortion but were denied one."

The reason for the ubiquity of abortion is, in part, its universal availability. Abortion is legal through all 9 months of pregnancy in all 50 states. In 1973, *Roe vs. Wade* established the right to abort, but *Doe vs. Bolton* ruled that no abortion could be prohibited if sought to terminate a pregnancy which threatens a woman's health. The Court defined "health" so broadly as to include "emotional, psychological, familial, and . . . age . . ." related factors, which made it functionally impossible for any government to prohibit any abortion. It should also be noted that the "Supremacy Clause" of the U.S. Constitution nullifies state law to the contrary. Additionally, these abortions are provided through a highly extensive system of extermination.

The Guttmacher Institute also reports that 16 states fund Medicaid abortions without restriction, and the foregoing *U.S. News* article reveals that the privately operated National Network of Abortion Funds finances abortions through 57 accounts in 29 states.

The apparatus which exterminates unborn children can't get much more "systematic" than that.

Clarifying Definitional Confusion

It is easy, however, to understand why there is so much confusion over the definition of the word "genocide." The *Cambridge International Dictionary of English*, Cambridge University Press, 1996, defines genocide as: "The murder of a whole group of people, esp. a whole nation, race, religious group, etc." The "etc." with which the definition ends emphasizes the evolving nature of the criteria by which victim classes are defined. But this definition's reference to the murder of "whole" groups and nations was already obsolete as it was being published.

Pol Pot's murder of 1 out of every 4 Cambodians is invariably described as "genocide" despite the fact that the perpetrators shared the same ethnicity and nationality as their victims and were not trying to kill "a whole nation." They only attempted to murder Cambodians deemed a threat to the Khmer Rouge revolution.

Time magazine, August 16, 1999, reports on the trials of Khmer Rouge leaders in Cambodia:

> Since Pol Pot eliminated all those with education or knowledge of the outside world, Phnom Penh became a city of country people, as well as a city of orphans and you still cannot find doctors or teachers or lawyers of a certain age.

And dictionary definitions of genocide have little to do with total numbers of victims. The recent killings of "only" 1 out every 20 Bosnians were widely described as "genocide" despite constituting only a small fraction of the numbers of European Jews (3 out of every 4) slaughtered in the Holocaust. Six million Jews died in all, but by 1998, at least 38 million unborn children have been killed in this country just since 1973.

Is Abortion a Hate Crime?

Some might argue that abortion is not genocide because genocide is a mass "hate crime" and most aborting mothers don't "hate" their unborn children. That may be true (though immaterial) concerning mothers but it certainly isn't true of abortionists and abortion advocates. Margaret Sanger, the founder of Planned Parenthood, declared war on "unwanted" children with her motto, "every child a wanted child." Planned Parenthood of Minnesota/South Dakota, for instance, has run newspaper advertisements which read in part "BABIES ARE LOUD, SMELLY, AND EXPENSIVE. UNLESS YOU WANT ONE. 1-800-230-PLAN." This hate-filled attack on "unwanted" unborn babies is couched in the language of bigotry. This is the dehumanizing rhetoric of genocide. Substitute for the word "babies" the name of any racial group and every mainstream newspaper in the country would rightly reject this mean-spirited ad.

This relentless, hateful, propaganda assault against "unwanted" unborn children has now been merged with overt racism. On August 9th, 1999, the Associated Press reported a story headlined "Study suggests link between crime drop, legal abortions," with a sub-headline which said "Researchers conclude that unwanted children are the most likely to break the law."

> The authors also conclude that unwanted children are most likely to commit crimes as adults and those most likely to give birth to unwanted children are teen-agers, minorities and the poor. Those are also the people most likely to choose abortion, the study found. . . .

> Judge Richard Posner, chief judge of the 7th U.S. Court of Appeals in Chicago called it ". . . a demonstration of the common-sensical point that unwanted children are quite likely not to turn out to be the best citizens."

Is the judge saying that a high percentage of racial minorities don't turn out to be "the best citizens"? Would he advocate the killing of "unwanted" minority newborn children? How does he feel about killing "unwanted" minority children butchered in the process of being born (as in "partial-birth" abortion)? Where and why would he draw the age line in targeting minority children for genocide?

Should the phrase "hate crime" be defined by the character of the "feelings" a perpetrator harbors toward his victim or the nature of the "behavior" by which he victimizes? A *New York Times* article, appearing in the August 13, 1999, *Orange County Register*, reported the publication of the memoirs of Adolph Eichmann, the SS official who oversaw the deportation and murder of millions of Jews during World War II. He also promoted the use of gas chambers in the death camps. The sub-headline for the article reads: "The Nazi who led Germany's genocide against Jews contended obedience, not hate guided him." Surely the fact that he didn't "hate" his victims (if true) would make him no less guilty of monumental hate crimes.

Did Slave Owners Hate Blacks?

Slavery and the legacy of "Jim Crow" was also an extremely "hateful" form of genocide but slave-owner Thomas Jefferson rationalized that he "loved" his slaves. On Jefferson's "kindness" toward them, author Virginius Dabney quotes Edmund Bacon, overseer at Monticello from 1806 to 1822, in his book *The Jefferson Scandals, A Rebuttal*: "Mr. Jefferson . . . would not allow them to be overworked and he would hardly ever allow one of them to be whipped." How's that for "love?". . .

In his 1953 book *The Constitutional Principles of Thomas Jefferson*, Caleb Perry Patterson argues that Jefferson was caught up in astounding self-justification:

> . . . it was Jefferson's humane feeling for his slaves that kept him from freeing them. To free the ordinary slave was not very different from starting him on the road to starvation. Or as Jefferson put it . . . like abandoning children.

Would Jefferson's "humane feeling" for his slaves make slavery any less a crime against humanity?

Reprinted by permission of Chuck Asay and Creators Syndicate. © Creators Syndicate, Inc.

Merrill D. Peterson adds in *Thomas Jefferson And The New Nation* that ". . . to turn loose the mass of slaves would have been, in his eyes, an act of heartless cruelty." What could be more "heartless" and "cruel" than slavery? Yet Jefferson's greed drove him to such self delusion that he saw its repudiation as "an act of heartless cruelty." This is not, of course, unlike the supposed "duty to abort" "unwanted" children in order to spare them lives of "hardship." Never mind that it is the selfish desires of born people which really motivate the "magnanimous" killing of the unborn. And so it was with Jefferson's oppression of his slaves. But Jefferson was as embarrassed by his avarice as are today's pro-aborts.

Dumas Malone, in his book *The Sage of Monticello*, describes the head games Jefferson played with the euphemisms he employed to rationalize his ownership of slaves:

> He resented the designation of these unfortunate human beings as property. He did not even like to call them slaves. When referring to those in his own possession, he generally spoke of them as servants or as his "people."

The dream world quality of Jefferson's self-serving rhetoric calls to mind awkard feminist references to "pregnancy termination" as they refuse to even say the word "abortion."

Jefferson fantasized an obligation to brutalize blacks. Virginius Dabney quotes in *The Jefferson Scandals, A Rebuttal*, an 1811 letter from Jefferson to John Lynch stating that ". . . to emancipate one's Negroes would be a betrayal of duty, since only a few exceptional slaves could fend for themselves." This is precisely the argument made by self-conscious pro-aborts who demand the deaths of fetuses who "might be born into poverty and thereby burden society."

It is cold comfort to an aborted baby that his mother didn't "hate" him.

Humanity and Personhood Defined

There is, of course, a consensus in the scientific community that human life begins at the instant a human egg is fertilized by a human sperm. The widely used 1998 medical textbook *The Developing Human, Clinically Oriented Embryology*, states at page 2 that "The intricate processes by which a baby develops from a single cell are miraculous. . . . This cell [the zygote] results from the union of an oocyte [egg] and sperm. A zygote is the beginning of a new human being. . . ." At page 18 this theme is repeated: "*Human development begins at fertilization* [emphasis in original]. . . ."

"Humanity," however, is quite different from "personhood." As seen above, the humanity of the unborn child is a matter of objective science. Personhood, however, is a legal status which society can confer upon or withhold from a class of human beings as a function of the subjective values which inform our "politics." In the medical ethics text entitled *Abortion, Medicine and the Law*, personhood is discussed in the context of the U.S. Supreme Court's decision in *Roe vs. Wade*, ". . . [T]he Court specifically repudiated the claim that fetuses are persons within the meaning of the fourteenth amendment. . . ."

We, therefore, know when life begins but we must decide at what point in the development of that life, we, as a society, will confer *rights of personhood*, the most fundamental of which is the right to not be slaughtered. The competing developmental points at which society might grant personhood include fertilization of the ovum, implantation of the blastocyst, viability of the fetus (ability to survive outside the uterus), birth, or the passage of some period following birth (in his book *Practical Ethics*, Peter Singer of Princeton University shockingly advocates the denial of personhood until one month following a child's birth).

So terms such as zygote, blastocyst, embryo, fetus, newborn, toddler, adolescent, adult, etc. merely describe arbitrarily defined stages in the biological development of a human life. But the inclusiveness with which we extend rights of personhood defines our collective morality. Are we greedy or generous? Are we brutal or compassionate?

Dominant societies have traditionally been selfish in the way they grant personhood. Ours is no exception. When a vulnerable group gets in our way or has something we want, we tend to define personhood in terms which exclude them. Indians got in the way of Westward settlement so we said they were subhuman to justify taking their land. We wanted the uncompensated work product of blacks so we said they were subhuman to justify taking their freedom. Unborn children have gotten in the way of our "liberation" so we say they are subhuman to justify taking their lives. . . .

The Holocaust and Abortion

Orthodox Jewish Rabbi Yehuda Levin of Brooklyn, New York, a prominent pro-life activist, agrees that abortion is genocide. He says that it can fairly be compared to the

Holocaust, lynchings and every other crime against humanity. The rabbi argues that:

> Each form of genocide, whether Holocaust, lynching, abortion, etc., differs from all the others in the motives and methods of its perpetrators. But each form of genocide is identical to all the others in that it involves the systematic slaughter, as state sanctioned "choice," of innocent, defenseless victims—while denying their "personhood."

When asked by the press what he thought of the GAP display on a university campus on which he was recently speaking, Holocaust survivor and Nobel laureate Elie Wiesel said, "I feel that it's wrong. Once you start comparing, everyone loses." Perhaps Mr. Wiesel has never read Dr. Martin Luther King's 1963 "Letter From a Birmingham Jail," which compared the brutalization of Jews in Germany with the brutalization of Blacks in America. In it, the great civil rights leader built on the consensus that the Holocaust wasn't mere evil, it was intolerable evil. Dr. King helped create a similar consensus that the savagery of segregation wasn't merely immoral. It was as intolerably immoral as the extermination of Jews. Our GAP pictures merely extend the logic of Dr. King's comparison to help people of conscience understand that the victimization of an unborn child can't fairly be trivialized as a nominal evil. It is an intolerable evil whose immensity is comparable to that of any other crime against humanity.

Jewish columnist Ben Stein echoes this sentiment in the May 1998 issue of *American Spectator* magazine:

> . . . [Pro-abortionists] cannot look at their handiwork or the handiwork they defend. Across the country, they shrink from photos of the babies killed in abortions. Through their mighty political groups, the pro-abortionists compel TV stations to refuse advertisements showing partial birth and other abortion artifacts. They will not even allow viewers (or themselves, I suspect) to see what their policies have wrought. They are, at least to my mind, like the Germans who refused to think about what was happening at Dachau and then vomited when they saw—and never wanted to see again. . . .

Genocide and the Myth of "Choice"

Many Americans defend "choice" by denying that they are "pro-abortion." They assert that they are actually "personally opposed" to abortion but don't believe they have the right to impose that "choice" on others. But most people who refuse to legislate morality on abortion, will rightly outlaw the "choice" to brutalize African Americans. The effort to outlaw abortion, like the campaign to outlaw racial injustice, isn't merely about personal morality. It is not merely about what a person *does*. It is about what a person does to another person.

The government *should* stay out of people's bedrooms (at least until abortions start being performed there), but government neutrality on genocide is a myth, whether the victim class is defined in terms of age (as in abortion), race, ethnicity or religion, etc. If the government suddenly withdrew legal protections for African Americans, would the government be "staying out of race," or would it be taking the side of those who think the lynching of African Americans should be a matter of "personal choice"? Such governmental "neutrality" would obviously abandon blacks to renewed genocide. (A "Whites Only" Web site asserted on the Internet that John William King, convicted of lynching African American James Bird, Jr. by dragging him to death behind a pickup truck in Jasper, Texas, was guilty only of "animal cruelty," according to *Newsweek*, March 8, 1999).

Would a person be seizing the moral high ground by saying "I am personally opposed to lynching blacks, I just don't think lynching blacks should be against the law"? Would the "moderate," progressive position on race be to say "I don't advocate the lynching of blacks but I do believe in the right to lynch blacks"? Neither is it "moderate" or progressive to make that argument against unborn children. . . .

Others deny that abortion is genocide by insisting that the Holocaust and lynchings were "murder" and abortion is "choice." They say this because they believe Jews and blacks are "persons" but unborn children are not. Those who murdered Jews and blacks, however, denied the personhood of their victims just as vehemently as practitioners of abortion deny the personhood of the unborn. . . .

Changing the Subject

The pictures of The Genocide Awareness Project (GAP) are sometimes condemned for supposedly creating an atmosphere conducive to the commission of anti-abortion violence. This fiction persists despite the widely known fact that GAP's sponsor, The Center For Bio-Ethical Reform (CBR), condemns violence against abortion providers—and against the babies killed by abortion providers.

Dr. Martin Luther King was often castigated by racists who unjustly blamed him for the violent unrest which sometimes followed his peaceful but confrontational demonstrations. Mayor Richard Daley of Chicago argued that if Dr. King would stop exposing racial injustice, black people would be less likely to participate in the riots which left many dead and injured. In his "Letter From a Birmingham Jail," Dr. King rebutted this dishonest attempt to change the subject:

> In your statement you asserted that our actions, though peaceful, must be condemned because they precipitate violence. . . . [I]t is immoral to urge an individual to withdraw his efforts to gain . . . basic constitutional rights because the quest precipitates violence. . . . Nonviolent direct action seeks to create such a crisis and establish such a creative tension that a community . . . is forced to confront the issue. It seeks so to dramatize the issue that it can no longer be ignored.

In a speech delivered just months before he would be murdered, he restated the imperative of confronting a complacent culture:

> . . . [U]ntil our problem is solved, America may have many, many days, but they will be full of trouble. There will be no rest, there will be no tranquillity in this country until the nation comes to terms with our problem.

Neither will there be tranquillity until the nation comes to terms with the "problem" of abortion.

| *"To compare abortion to the real genocide of real people is highly insulting to the relatives and descendants of slaves and Holocaust victims."*

Abortion Is Not a Form of Genocide

Joyce Arthur

In the following viewpoint, Joyce Arthur contends that abortion is not, as some commentators have claimed, a form of genocide. Genocide, she points out, entails the intentional destruction of an ethnic group or an act of hatred against a specific community of people. Abortion, however, is a legal medical procedure that expands women's reproductive options, enabling them to improve their own lives as well as the lives of their families. Arthur also maintains that most anti-abortionists do not truly believe abortion is a form of genocide, or else they would take much stronger action against pro-choice advocates. Arthur, a spokesperson for the Pro-Choice Action Network in Vancouver, Canada, edits the Canadian newsletter *Pro-Choice Press*.

As you read, consider the following questions:
1. According to Arthur, what images are depicted in the Center for Bio-Ethical Reform's Genocide Awareness Project?
2. Why do women have abortions, in the author's opinion?
3. In Arthur's view, what is sexist about the "abortion-as-genocide mentality"?

Reprinted from "Abortion Is Not a Form of Genocide," by Joyce Arthur, *The Humanist*, July/August 2000, by permission of the author.

Anti-abortion groups are fond of saying that abortion is a form of genocide, comparable to the Nazi Holocaust and other atrocities. This dubious proposition, offensive to many, outstrips even the more common anti-choice claim that abortion is murder. What is the underlying logic behind this outrageous abortion-as-genocide claim? Do those who make the charge really believe it? And what does it tell us about their view of women?

The Center for Bio-Ethical Reform

Let's look at the tactics of a particular anti-abortion group, the Center for Bio-Ethical Reform (CBR) founded in 1990, based in California, and headed by attorney Gregg Cunningham. CBR appears to be the leading promoter of the "abortion is genocide" mantra and has sponsored a high-profile campaign to educate North American young people about this new "truth."

Since 1998, about two dozen university campuses in Canada and the United States have been visited by CBR's controversial Genocide Awareness Project (GAP), a traveling roadshow. The GAP display consists of graphic six-by-thirteen-foot color billboards of Holocaust, black lynching, and other victims of real genocide juxtaposed with pictures of aborted fetuses. For example, one billboard reads, "The changing face of choice," with the first panel showing the bodies of Holocaust victims, the Nazi swastika, and the caption "Religious Choice." The second panel shows a lynched black man with the caption "Racial Choice," and the third shows an aborted fetus with the caption "Reproductive Choice." One billboard even compares Planned Parenthood to Nazis.

The stated goal of the GAP display is to make people think differently about abortion. But judging by what happens, the unstated goal is apparently to anger, offend, and incite violence—then use the ensuing publicity to make pro-choicers look bad. Many people find the graphic depiction of historical atrocities to be an extremely offensive way to advance an anti-abortion agenda. Indeed, CBR's own website features photographs of angry, distressed, and traumatized students viewing the display—although CBR insists it's solely the "horror" of abortion that's causing the upset.

Questionable Tactics

The GAP display also has been met with pro-choice counter-protests at almost every campus where it has appeared. On at least five campuses, violence and vandalism have occurred, with students attacking the displays or GAP staff members and volunteers. At Ohio State University, about thirty protesters rushed the display in an incident that Associated Press termed a "riot"; a female student was arrested after trying to slash a poster with a knife. At the University of Kansas, an African American student rammed the display with his truck and a female Jewish student physically assaulted a GAP staffer; both were arrested. As Cunningham vowed at one campus, "We will make an example out of lawbreakers."

In clear anticipation of such violence, CBR erects barricades to surround the display and shield its staff and volunteers. Incredibly, it demands that universities supply these steel fences as well as pay for the extraordinary cost of a campus police squad to stand guard. If the university balks at the expense, CBR threatens to sue—as happened at the University of British Columbia. In fact, CBR often announces its willingness to litigate. Indiana University is currently under just such a threat simply because it is trying to restrict the GAP display to the campus' designated free-speech area. And before the group even comes to a university, it sends what some call a "bully letter" to the administration spelling out CBR's constitutional rights. As Cunningham stated in the spring 2000 issue of the group's newsletter *In Perspective*, "Any university which attempts to interfere with the exercise of CBR's First Amendment rights will be sued."

Once on campus, CBR then gathers evidence for potential lawsuits and criminal investigations by routinely videotaping and photographing students at the display, especially pro-choice protesters. It has even been known to take photos and videos of vehicle license plates. Then, whenever violence or vandalism does occur, CBR is well equipped to sue or press charges. The group also milks favorable publicity out of any negative incident, condemning universities and pro-choice students for trying to restrict its free-speech rights.

Despite CBR's tactics, there is still the group's basic claim to consider. But is abortion genocide? Most people find this question absurdly offensive on its face. Yet when I surfed the Internet to find pro-choice responses, I found almost nothing. The reason, I suspect, is that most reasonable people can't be bothered to refute something so obviously preposterous and don't wish to dignify it with a reply. Or perhaps it's because, as Mark Twain said, "A lie can travel halfway around the world while the truth is still putting on its shoes." In any case, given CBR's activism, I'm convinced a rebuttal is long overdue.

To start, it must be said that to compare abortion to the real genocide of real people is highly insulting to the relatives and descendants of slaves and Holocaust victims. The term genocide was coined by Raphael Lemkin in 1944 to mean "the destruction of a nation or an ethnic group." Its definition has since legitimately expanded to include any violent and intolerable act of hatred against a particular community of people. It is an inexcusable crime. Abortion, by contrast, is an essential, legal, medical procedure that women need to have available, not only to give them control over their bodies and lives but to preserve and improve the lives of their families. Women have abortions not out of hatred or selfish convenience or because they're coerced into it but generally because they want to be good mothers to their existing or possible children.

However, in CBR's twenty-eight-page pamphlet *Why Abortion Is Genocide*—available at GAP displays and, in slightly edited form, on the CBR website—Cunningham argues that the definition of genocide is broad enough to encompass fetuses and that "unwanted" fetuses are a dehumanized group comparable to black slaves, interned Jews, and Cambodian Killing Field victims.

Personhood Is Subjective

The first major flaw in this argument is the shaky premise that fetuses are full human beings with the same status and rights thereof. This fails to recognize that fetuses are completely dependent on a woman's body to survive and that the fetal mode of growth and survival fits the technical definition of parasite—notwithstanding Cunningham's opinion of that word as a dehumanizing slur. It also fails to recognize that pregnant women would be forced to forfeit their own human rights in exchange for fetal rights. In Cunningham's view, fetuses are vulnerable persons being exterminated because they've gotten in the way of selfish "women's liberation" (Cunningham's quotation marks).

Clearly, the supposed personhood of a fetus is a matter of subjective opinion that can't be conclusively agreed upon by law, science, or society in general. This is why the term genocide can't refer to unborn fetuses that aren't yet legal members of society and don't yet have undisputed personhood. This is why only born babies should have full human rights under the law and why we must leave the abortion decision up to the individual woman's conscience.

Paradoxically, Cunningham unwittingly draws attention to the subjectivity of fetal personhood when he notes with shock and horror that Peter Singer, author of the book *Practical Ethics*, advocates the denial of personhood until one month after a child's birth. Perhaps Cunningham, a devout Christian, should have noticed that the God of the Bible seems to hold the same opinion. Instructing Moses on how to conduct a census, God says in Numbers 3:40 to count only those firstborn males "a month old and upward," implying that those younger aren't true persons. Of course, one could say that this is only a subjective opinion shared by Singer and God, but most devout Christians don't take such a casual attitude toward what they consider divine precept.

Infringing on a Woman's Human Rights

The second major flaw in the argument is that it completely ignores the serious infringement on women's human rights if safe, legal abortion were to be taken away. If abortion were stopped, what would be left? A double "genocide"!—that of countless women undergoing unsafe, illegal abortions, accompanied by only a small decline in actual abortion rates. Most "unwanted babies" would go right on being aborted, and there would be nothing Cunningham or any other anti-abortion advocate could do about it. Abortion is a universal practice, occurring in every society and throughout history, regardless of laws. Therefore, the anti-abortion movement's naive opposition to it may be a far stronger indication of misogyny than of a concern for "unborn babies." And abortion being illegal doesn't just kill women, it also negates their moral autonomy, cripples their economic independence, criminalizes them for their biology, and generally turns them into all-around second-class citizens.

On the positive side, Cunningham does briefly reference in his pamphlet the history of women's oppression, including rape, to show that women also have been victims of "genocide." But in the context of abortion he mentions women only twice—once to call them "victims" of abortion who nevertheless must be deeply "ashamed of their conduct" and once to label them "narcissistic" and "spiteful" for having abortions instead of putting their babies up for adoption. What shocking disrespect and lack of compassion for both women and babies! Why are women who have abortions automatically thought of as shame-filled victims instead of independent moral agents? Why are women's concern and anguish for the children they give up so irrelevant? And since when are babies commodities that women should produce for the procurement of others?

A Deep-Rooted Sexism

In fact, underlying the entire abortion-as-genocide mentality lies a deep-rooted sexism. Cunningham and most other anti-abortion activists seem to be largely unaware of it, but the following thought experiment should help bring it to light.

For argument's sake, let's say that the Genocide Awareness Project is correct in saying that abortion is genocide. This begs the obvious question: who bears the responsibility for this genocide? Who should go on trial for these crimes against humanity? The answer depends on how you view the nature and status of women.

Most people in our society believe that women shouldn't be limited by law or tradition to the sole role of bearing and rearing children. Most believe that women deserve equal opportunity and respect in the public sphere. They believe that women are autonomous beings with the brains and the right to make their own decisions about their lives. If one believes these things, then women bear full responsibility for the abortions they choose to have. If abortion is genocide then women must be genocidal murderers. That is why many people, including myself, consider the GAP display to be hate propaganda against women.

But do anti-abortionists, in fact, blame women for abortion? Not generally. In spite of all their rhetoric about abortion being murder, they rarely blame those who, following this reasoning, are the murderers. Instead they attack doctors and clinics and dump their condemnation at the doors of Planned Parenthood, politicians, judges, evolution, humanism, and our "culture of death."

Restrictions on Abortion

Today the right to abortion is still legal in the United States. But restrictive state laws and the attacks of anti-abortion forces are making it harder and harder for women to exercise this right. There are fewer doctors performing abortions. The result of this will mean that instead of going in early for a simple and safe medical procedure, many women will find themselves trapped—forced to wait for later and more difficult abortions, forced to bear unwanted children, or forced to swallow poisons, mutilate themselves with coat hangers, or die at the hands of fast-buck butchers. All this was routine in the United States prior to 1973 and continues to be routine in many parts of the world today.

Revolutionary Worker, January 15, 1995.

Partly, this is just practical—women are an impossibly large target, comprising half the population. Anti-abortionists can't very well throw tens of millions of women into prison. But should we really let people off the hook for committing genocide just because there are too many of them? (We can't cop out by comparing women to the German people during World War II who stood by and did nothing while the Nazis built and ran the death camps. In the case of abortion, according to CBR, it is women themselves who are committing and authorizing the deed.)

Does the anti-choice willingness to overlook women's responsibility for abortion stem perhaps from a deep compassion for women? No. Those against legal abortion aren't really interested in helping real women live real lives; their main goal is to outlaw abortion again. And we know all too well the tragic toll of illegal abortion on women's lives, health, and rights. Yet anti-abortionists claim that by stopping abortion they will actually be helping women. This apparent contradiction is easily resolved with the realization that anti-abortionists truly believe that women are *victims* of legal abortion.

Here's where another view about the nature and status of women comes in—a view that seems to be held by most anti-choice people. They believe that women's natural, primary role is to have and rear children. (Many even believe that women who want something more or different than having a family are deviant.) They believe that women are easily victimized by circumstances and easily led by other people. They believe that women aren't ultimately responsible for their actions because, like children, they need direction and moral guidance. If these beliefs are true, women do not bear responsibility for their abortions; they have been misled into having them by the society and people around them (except for those "deviant" women, of course). Society itself becomes the genocidal murderer, with abortion providers and pro-choice politicians serving as scapegoats.

The Rationalizations of Anti-Choice Women

Obviously, people who hold such a patronizing and traditional view of women's nature would have difficulty empathizing with the horrible, gut recognition of others that the Genocide Awareness Project is actually hate propaganda against women. Anti-abortion students who invite GAP onto their campuses are a case in point, since they don't seem to understand what all the fuss is about. What makes this especially sad is that many of these students are women themselves. I can conclude only that such young women don't really believe in their hearts that women are entitled to, able to, or want to make important decisions about their lives.

This insight into the anti-choice view of women's nature helps explain a strange phenomenon that regularly plagues abortion clinics: anti-abortion women having abortions. Planned Parenthood of America estimates that about 15 percent of abortions are performed on conservative Christian women—many of them anti-choice.

I've been collecting stories from abortion providers across North America that describe the antics and rationalizations of anti-abortion women who need abortions. Some clinics actually have a policy of refusing, for liability reasons, to perform abortions on anti-abortion women. This is because these women tend to have great difficulty taking ownership of their abortions and often place the "blame" on anyone but themselves—usually the doctor or clinic. This can result in repressed emotions that manifest themselves later in the form of lawsuits against the clinic. Sadly, these women have bought into the sexist (and neurotic) notion that they're not personally responsible for their actions. Here's one example, in a clinic director's own words:

> We saw a woman who, after four attempts and many hours of counseling both at the hospital and our clinic, finally, calmly and uneventfully had her abortion. Four months later, she called me on Christmas Eve to tell me that she was not and never was pro-choice and that we failed to recognize that she was clinically depressed at the time of her abortion. The purpose of her call was to chastise me for not sending her off to the psych unit instead of the procedure room.

Most clinics do perform abortions on anti-abortion women because they feel it is their obligation to help all women. However, much more thorough counseling is provided to ensure that the women understand their decision and take responsibility for it. As a result, some anti-abortion women do make peace with their abortions, and a few even become pro-choice—or at least more compassionate toward women who are pro-choice or who seek abortion services.

Unfortunately, many others rationalize their decision by convincing themselves that theirs is a unique case—not like those "other" women—even though they have abortions for the same sorts of reasons. Still others demand special treatment: for example, they ask to be let in the back door to avoid being seen by fellow protesters; they reject counseling because no one could "possibly understand" their situation; and they refuse to sit in the waiting room with those "slutty" women. Finally, some are delighted to have the opportunity to inform clinic staff and doctors that they are a bunch of "murderers," although the women usually wait until their abortion is over to say it.

Cynical Public Relations

On some level, a few anti-abortion activists do seem to recognize that women are responsible for their abortions. Some ultra-extremists are, in fact, quite willing to throw millions of women into prison, if necessary. Others—notably those associated with anti-abortion counseling agencies—are known to instill tremendous guilt in women for "killing their baby."

However, since women's accountability for abortion obviously isn't a major stumbling block for most in the anti-abortion movement, that reveals something else besides their narrow view of women's nature: anti-abortionists don't really believe that abortion is murder, let alone genocide. If they did, they surely would be far angrier at those responsible. Indeed, anti-abortion actions often reveal more than words. Randall Terry, founder of Operation Rescue, even felt forced to spell it out to his followers: "If you believe it's murder, act like it's murder!" A few followed his advice but most never did.

And if anti-abortionists really believed abortion is genocide and really believed their own proclamation that doctors are responsible, they wouldn't hero-worship a former abortion provider like Dr. Bernard Nathanson. Now anti-choice, Nathanson gets paid to talk at "pro-life" dinner parties about the 70,000 abortions he performed at his New York clinic in the 1970s. But surely genocide is an unforgivable crime, regardless of the perpetrator's remorse and repentance. Would the Nuremberg Trials have let Adolf Eichmann off the hook if he had apologized for engineering the Final Solution?

Clearly, the anti-abortion movement is far too quick to forgive and forget. This can only mean that its abortion-as-genocide campaign is nothing more than cynical public relations. Based upon faulty logic, a misogynist view of women, and profound disrespect for the victims of real genocide, the Genocide Awareness Project, in my view, is nothing more than an attack against human intellect, dignity, and ethics.

Periodical Bibliography

The following articles have been selected to supplement the diverse views presented in this chapter. Addresses are provided for periodicals not indexed in the *Readers' Guide to Periodical Literature*, the *Alternative Press Index*, the *Social Sciences Index*, or the *Index to Legal Periodicals and Books*.

Anonymous	"I Am an Abortion Doctor," *Ms.*, June/July 1999.
Lorena Rodrigues Bottum	"Ordinary Abortions," *Wall Street Journal*, March 12, 1999.
Christianity Today	"The Abortion Debate Is Over," December 6, 1999.
Johnny Hunter	"A Civil-Rights Movement to Save Unborn Children Is the Key to Ending the Scourge of Abortion," *Insight*, October 23, 2000. Available from 3600 New York Ave. NE, Washington, DC 20002.
Wendy Kaminer	"Abortion and Autonomy," *American Prospect*, June 5, 2000.
Heather King	"One Woman's Journey: Following My Own Unguided Will," *Commonweal*, May 3, 1996.
Frances Kissling	"The Vatican and the Politics of Reproductive Health," *USA Today*, May 1999.
J.M. Lawson Jr. and Ignacio Castuera	"We Should Trust Women to Do the Choosing," *Los Angeles Times*, June 23, 2000. Available from Reprints, Times Mirror Square, Los Angeles, CA 90053.
Peter J. Leithart	"Attacking the Tabernacle," *First Things*, November 1999. Available from 156 Fifth Ave., Suite 400, New York, NY 10010.
National Review	"Dead Reckoning," January 26, 1998.
Progressive	"*Roe v. Wade* at Twenty-five," February 1998.
Richard Shoenig	"The Idiot's Guide to Salvation," *Humanist*, January/February 2000.
Benjamin J. Stein	"A Golden Age for Thugs," *American Spectator*, May 1998.

CHAPTER 2

Should Abortion Rights Be Restricted?

Chapter Preface

Since 1973, a woman's right to an abortion has been protected by the Supreme Court. However, the court has also declared that states may impose certain kinds of regulations that limit access to surgical abortions. According to the National Abortion and Reproductive Rights Action League, a majority of states currently enforces at least one of the following restrictions: 24- to 48-hour waiting periods before women can undergo the procedure, counseling emphasizing the drawbacks of abortion, obligations for minors to notify their parents or obtain their consent before having an abortion, and bans on the procedure at public facilities.

Those who support these restrictions maintain that such statutes reflect the average American's concerns about abortion. Gallup polls, for example, reveal that more than 70 percent of Americans support a prohibition on abortion after the first trimester of pregnancy—including 46 percent of those who identify themselves as strongly pro-choice. While most citizens believe that abortion should be available during the first three months of pregnancy, many also agree that a woman should not have an abortion to avoid inconveniences such as interruptions to her education or career. Regulations on abortion, some argue, make it less likely that a woman will make a rushed or misguided decision.

Critics, however, point out that restrictions can force women to delay their abortions until later in pregnancy when the potential health risks are greater. "We're seeing an increase of second-trimester procedures because young women are delaying telling their parents," says clinician Susan Hill. Others contend that no one should have the right to interfere with a choice that is ultimately up to the woman. As commentator Elizabeth Schulte argues, "Passing even one restriction strengthens the idea that women shouldn't be allowed to make this decision by themselves, even though they must live with the consequences of an unwanted or dangerous pregnancy."

The question of restrictions on abortion rights has generated some of the most fervent dialogue in the ongoing abortion debate. The authors of the following chapter offer compelling opinions on this continuing controversy.

"If the courts would get out of the business of regulating abortion, most legislatures would pass laws reflecting the moderate views of the great majority."

Abortion Should Be Restricted

Michael W. McConnell

In the viewpoint that follows, Michael W. McConnell maintains that the Supreme Court's legalization of abortion is based on faulty reasoning. For example, the court has stated that a woman's decision to abort is based on a constitutional "right of privacy," yet no such right can be found in the Constitution, McConnell explains. The court also claims that it cannot resolve the question of when life begins, but it implicitly denies that the fetus is a person by refusing to protect its life. A majority of Americans, however, oppose abortions after the first trimester and support parental notification laws, waiting periods, and other moderate restrictions on abortion. The Supreme Court misrepresents the will of the people by allowing women to have abortions for any reason, the author concludes. McConnell is a professor of constitutional law at the University of Utah.

As you read, consider the following questions:
1. What percentage of pregnancies end in abortion, according to McConnell?
2. In the author's opinion, what "circular argument" can be found in the Supreme Court's decision to legalize abortion?
3. In McConnell's view, why do judges have no real basis for overturning legislative regulations on abortion?

On January 22, 1973, the U.S. Supreme Court handed down its decision legalizing abortion throughout the country. The day before *Roe v. Wade*, abortion was flatly illegal in almost all states, though a few had recently relaxed their laws. On the day after *Roe*, women suddenly had a constitutional right to get an abortion for any reason, a right that effectively applied at any time during the nine months of pregnancy. (In theory, states could still ban abortion in the last three months unless it was necessary for the health of the woman—but the court defined "health" so broadly as to make this limitation meaningless.) The number of abortions quickly soared to almost 1.5 million every year, roughly 30% of all pregnancies.

Roe v. Wade is the most enduringly controversial court decision of the twentieth century, and rightly so. Rather than putting the issue to rest, the court converted it into the worst sort of political struggle—one involving angry demonstrators, nasty confirmation battles and confrontational sound bites. With ordinary politicians, who are masters of compromise, out of the picture, the issue became dominated by activists of passionate intensity on both extremes of the spectrum.

A Time for Controversy

Controversial decisions—even decisions that rend the body politic—are sometimes necessary. The Constitution stands for certain fundamental principles of free government, and there are times when the courts must intervene to make sure they are not neglected. But when judges act on the basis of their own political predilections, without regard to constitutional text or the decisions of representative institutions, the results are illegitimate.

The reasoning of *Roe v. Wade* is an embarrassment to those who take constitutional law seriously, even to many scholars who heartily support the outcome of the case. As John Hart Ely, former dean of Stanford Law School and a supporter of abortion rights, has written, *Roe* "is *not* constitutional law and gives almost no sense of an obligation to try to be."

The court's reasoning proceeded in two steps. First, it found that a "right of privacy" exists under the Constitution, and that this right is "broad enough to encompass a woman's decision whether or not to terminate her pregnancy." Since this meant that the right to abortion is constitutionally protected, a state could interfere with the right only if it has a "compelling state interest" for doing so.

But the right of privacy is nowhere mentioned in the Constitution. Various judges, according to the court, had found "at least the roots of that right" in the First Amendment, in the "penumbras of the Bill of Rights," in the Ninth Amendment or in the "concept of liberty guaranteed by the first section of the Fourteenth Amendment." This vague statement is tantamount to confessing the court did not much care where in the Constitution this supposed right might be found. All that mattered was it be "broad enough" to encompass abortion.

A Nebulous "Right"

Even assuming a right of privacy can be excavated from somewhere, anywhere, in the Constitution, what does it mean? The court avoided defining the term, except by giving examples from previous cases. The trouble is, counterexamples abound. The federal "right of privacy" has never been held to protect against laws banning drug use, assisted suicide or even consensual sodomy—just to mention a few examples of crimes that are no less "private" than abortion. It is impossible to know what does and does not fall within this nebulous category.

Even assuming that there is a right of privacy, and that its contours can be discerned from the court's examples, surely it must be confined to activities that affect no one else. It would be an odd kind of privacy that confers the power to inflict injury on nonconsenting third parties. Yet the entire rationale for antiabortion laws is that an abortion *does* inflict injury on a nonconsenting third party, the fetus. It is not possible to describe abortion as a "privacy right" without first concluding that the fetus does not count as a third party with protectable interests.

An Unresolvable Issue?

That brings us to step two in the court's argument. Far from resolving the thorny question of when a fetus is another person deserving of protection—surely the crux of the privacy right, if it exists—the justices determined that the issue is unresolvable. They noted that there has been a "wide divergence of thinking" regarding the "most sensitive and difficult question" of "when life begins." They stated that "[w]hen those trained in the respective disciplines of medicine, philosophy, and theology are unable to arrive at any consensus, the judiciary . . . is not in a position to speculate as to the answer."

Reprinted by permission of Chuck Asay and Creators Syndicate. © Creators Syndicate, Inc.

According to the court, the existence of this uncertainty meant that the state's asserted interest in protecting unborn life could not be deemed "compelling." But this leaves us with an entirely circular argument. The supposed lack of consensus about when life begins is important because when state interests are uncertain they cannot be "compelling"; and a compelling state interest is required before the state can limit a constitutional right. But the constitutional right in question ("privacy") only exists if the activity in question does not abridge the rights of a non-consenting third party—the very question the court says cannot be resolved.

If it cannot be resolved, there is no way to determine whether abortion is a "right of privacy."

In any event, the court's claim that it was not resolving the issue of "when life begins" was disingenuous. In our system, all people are entitled to protection from killing and other forms of private violence. The court can deny such protection to fetuses only if it presupposes they are not persons.

One can make a pretty convincing argument, however, that fetuses *are* persons. They are alive; their species is *Homo sapiens*. They are not simply an appendage of the mother; they have a separate and unique chromosomal structure. Surely, before beings with all the biological characteristics of humans are stripped of their rights as "persons" under the law, we are entitled to an explanation of why they fall short. For the court to say it cannot "resolve the difficult question of when life begins" is not an explanation.

Eliminating Legislative Deliberation

It is true, of course, that people honestly disagree about the question of when life begins. But divergence of opinion is not ordinarily a reason to take a decision away from the people and their elected representatives. One of the functions of democratic government is to provide a forum for debating and ultimately resolving controversial issues. Judges cannot properly strike down the acts of the political branches that do not clearly violate the Constitution. If no one knows when life begins, the courts have no basis for saying the legislature's answer is wrong. To be sure, abortion is an explosive issue, with noisy and self-righteous advocates on both sides. But the Supreme Court made it far more so by eliminating the possibility of reasoned legislative deliberation and prudent compromise.

It is often said that abortion is an issue that defies agreement or compromise. But if the polling data are correct, there has been a broad and surprisingly stable consensus among the American people for at least the past 30 years that rejects the uncompromising positions of both pro-choice and pro-life advocates. Large majorities (61% in a recent *New York Times*/CBS poll) believe that abortion should be legally available during the early months of pregnancy. There is also widespread support for legal abortions when the reasons are sufficiently weighty (rape, incest, probability of serious birth defect, serious danger to the mother's health).

But only 15% believe that abortion should generally be available *after* the first three months, when the fetus has developed a beating heart, fingers and toes, brain waves and a full set of internal organs. Majorities oppose abortions for less weighty reasons, such as avoiding career interruptions. Even larger majorities (approaching 80%) favor modest regulations, like waiting periods and parental consent requirements, to guard against hasty and ill-informed decisions. (The Supreme Court has permitted some such regulations to stand in the years since *Roe*.) Most Americans would prohibit particularly grisly forms of the procedure, like partial-birth abortions.

Reject the Extremes

These opinions have persisted without significant change since the early 1970s, and are shared by women and men, young and old alike. On the question of abortion, Americans overwhelmingly reject the extremes. If the courts would get out of the business of regulating abortion, most legislatures would pass laws reflecting the moderate views of the great majority. This would provide more protection than the unborn have under current law, though probably much less than pro-life advocates would wish.

The Supreme Court brought great discredit on itself by overturning state laws regulating abortion without any persuasive basis in constitutional text or logic. And to make matters worse, it committed these grave legal errors in the service of an extreme vision of abortion rights that the vast majority of Americans rightly consider unjust and immoral. *Roe v. Wade* is a useful reminder that government by the representatives of the people is often more wise, as well as more democratic, than rule by lawyers in robes.

"Roe [v. Wade] *stated that choice is a constitutional right, just like our other basic freedoms.*"

Abortion Should Not Be Restricted

Don Sloan

In the following viewpoint, Don Sloan bemoans the fact that women are finding it increasingly difficult to obtain legal abortions. Although the Supreme Court's 1973 *Roe v. Wade* decision supposedly protects a woman's right to a safe abortion, the majority of counties in the United States have no abortion facilities, and women often face restrictive measures such as mandatory counseling sessions, twenty-four-hour waiting periods, or parental notification laws. Sloan maintains that such restrictions impinge upon a woman's legal right to choose. The decision to abort a fetus may be an unpleasant option, but reproductive choice is ultimately about rights and freedoms, not morals and ethics, the author asserts. Sloan is a physician and an assistant editor of *Political Affairs*, a monthly periodical.

As you read, consider the following questions:

1. According to Sloan, what percentage of abortions occur in the first trimester of pregnancy?
2. What are some of the inflammatory terms anti-choice activists use to chastise those who support the right to choose, according to the author?
3. In Sloan's view, what are the four basic truths about the abortion debate?

Reprinted, with permission, from "Basic Issues in the Abortion Debate," by Don Sloan, *Political Affairs*, July 1999.

S he's young, unmarried, working at a marginal job, barely making ends meet—and very much pregnant. She doesn't have the vacation and sick-time perks that would allow for time off. Family leave doesn't apply in her case. Queasy every morning, she is worried how long her boss will tolerate her tardiness. Single and nearly jobless, she's at wit's end.

Her local hospital doesn't do abortions. If she had the bucks, she could go off to the big city somewhere, a clinic, or even a private doctor. No, it has to be here and it has to be now—time is running out. So she gets a name—a nurse, a pharmacist, maybe a retired health care worker. That's if she's in luck. If her luck has run out, she ends up without any name at all and finds herself in some hospital emergency room, bleeding, in shock, in a coma—dead.

A cautionary tale from the '50s? Hardly. Unless living in a major city, women today face the de facto prohibition of abortion entitled by law. The right to a clean, safe procedure is theoretically protected by that law, at least for the time being. In practice, however, it is a right that is becoming more and more difficult to exercise.

Anti-Abortion Maneuvering

Although both the American College of Obstetricians and Gynecologists (ACOG) and the American Medical Association (AMA) seem to have sidestepped the real issues of the abortion question, they are on the public record as being officially pro-choice. Early abortion is still ten times safer than childbirth, so from a purely medical standpoint, choice is the position that gives the doctor the greatest latitude to do what is best for the patient—if that is what the patient chooses. But when it gets down to individual cases, there's nothing to stop doctors or hospital administrations from playing politics and branding physicians who do abortions.

Infighting, controversy, and political maneuvering go on within the sterile walls of the medical world perhaps as much as on the floors of the legislature or on the sidewalks in front of abortion clinics. The term "abortionist" still carries with it a heavy weight. We've made it legal, but we haven't yet made it respectable—not quite.

First-trimester abortion, making up almost 90 percent of

all procedures, is "minor" surgery in the lexicon of the gynecologist. Despite its nominal status it is still subjected to disproportionately close scrutiny. Several years ago a research study exposed the way various health-care professionals, from doctors to hospital clerks, viewed the procedure. The study compared how intake emergency room services handled women who sought help for what were allegedly complaints or complications following either an abortion or a dilatation and curettage (D&C) (a carbon-copy procedure done for reasons other than to end pregnancy). The results were startling.

With rare exceptions, abortion patients came under greater surveillance than D&C patients. The former underwent more extensive evaluations, including lab testing, x-rays, and (usually unnecessary) additional surgery, often of a major type involving abdominal incisions and even hysterectomy.

The researchers concluded there was an obvious prejudice against abortion patients and the procedure itself, partly due to ignorance on the part of the staff or out of a regressive attitude which looks down upon patients and their doctors.

A Time Bomb

In the abortion equation, it is the doctors, still mostly male, who are being stigmatized as the culprits more so than the patients. In states that are waiting for the next test of *Roe v. Wade*, the criminal penalties are aimed at the physicians, with an added wrist-slapping for the patients. As a result, anger against them has led to the brutal killing of a physician in Florida and his colleague and the shooting of another in Kansas. Most recently is the sniper murder of a highly respected practitioner in Buffalo, New York. . . . These are the inevitable outcomes of the policies of past administrations in Washington which, turning a blind eye to the attitudes and escalating violence of anti-choice forces, inadvertently triggered what was a time bomb waiting to explode.

The seeds of violence have been sown in the semantics of those who purport to oppose killing. But in this case, the pen is as mighty as the sword, as anti-choice rhetoric only serves to further obfuscate the issues. To irresponsibly label an accepted procedure a "murder" of a "child" in defiance of law and medicine is to castigate those who perform this task as "murderers." In this twisted revision of the terms of debate, pro-choice has become pro-abortion. Pro-abortion, anti-life. Anti-choice then becomes pro-life and it filters down to an option between life or abortion, now synonymous for death. And abortion, "a murder by murderers," is performed not for a woman to remove an unwanted pregnancy or embryo but instead on a "kid," an "unborn," "your baby." Names have even been assigned to these entities.

The revaluation of terms goes even further: the procedure is not being done in a hospital or outpatient unit, center, or clinic, but in a "killing chamber," "crematorium," or "vacuum station." Specially-made videos have been produced depicting the movement of the embryo as that of a playful tot, seemingly communicating with its future parents, family, and friends.

Some Basic Truths

The time has come to stop this word play demagogy. I offer instead four basic truths:

First, that the "abortion" debate is a misnomer; we are not debating abortion, we are debating rights. Rights, not morals; rights, not ethics. *Roe v. Wade*, the law of the United States, is in effect. That is why Pennsylvania's *Casey* (*Casey v. Planned Parenthood*) decision requiring a 24-hour delay was nothing more than pure politics. *Roe* stated that choice is a constitutional right, just like our other basic freedoms. Would any libertarian agree to forcing a day's delay before exercising the freedom of, say, speech? Or a required session and an overnight consultation with a government-appointed counselor before deciding in which church to worship? Or perhaps a compulsory hour-long discussion with the news-stand proprietor on the relative merits of various publications before making a purchase?

Second, life and its inception are considerations for science to solve, not religion. A most cherished American tenet is the separation of church and state. The class action *Doe* case (*Doe v. Bolton*), after much authoritative testimony, has set a 24-week limit as the time when, as has been taught to gynecologists for generations, the embryo becomes a fetus and independent life is plausible. Speaking of potential children is analogous to an acorn being a potential oak tree or a grape being a potential bottle of fine champagne. *Roe* and *Doe* have had their rulings bent, not broken.

Infringing on Women's Rights

Third, that right and that science are being denied to a majority group who have been the victims of male dominance since time immemorial—women. Choice is clearly a battle over male supremacy and class domination and control. To deny that abortion is about women and their rights and freedoms is to behave like the ostrich that keeps its head in the sand.

Fourth, the abortion/choice question is but an extension of what health care in America is for women. The U.S. remains the world's only industrialized nation without a universal health care program. It has even become a message of our foreign policy.

The conservative coalition's influence has channeled funding of the United States Agency for International Development (USAID), the agency responsible for health care in developing countries away from abortion even in those areas where it is legal. Bill Clinton's tacit reversal of that policy has not resulted in substantial changes.

Cumbersome Restrictions

"Permit but discourage" has been proposed as an alternative to choice. Under the *Casey* and before that the *Webster* (*Webster v. Reproductive Health Services*) decision, consent and waiting period restrictions are equal to an outright denial for many women, especially the young and the poor. As of now over 80 percent of the counties in the country have no abortion facilities or staff.

Suggesting that women need an additional waiting period flies in the face of common sense. It is as though this very heart-rending decision to abort were made on a whim by a woman on her way downtown to do a little shopping who just happened to pass by her local abortion emporium and decided to stop in and have one. It furthers the stereotype of a female as being muddleheaded, morally infantile, emotionally unstable, and weak. Does anyone really think women have abortions for the same reasons climbers scale mountains—because they are there? The decision to abort is always a true dilemma—one made between two unpleasant and unwanted alternatives.

No one is pro-abortion. No one is anti-life. No one. I don't think there is anyone doing abortions who hasn't wished at some point that the situations creating the demand for them would just go away, including me. There have been plenty of times when I've wanted to say, "Enough! This is more human tragedy than I want to deal with." But that would require a different world—one without poverty, rape, incest, contraceptive failure, genetic defects, maternal illnesses, unprotected moments of passion, or human fallibility.

Restrictions Erode Rights

Each and every restriction on legal abortion further erodes women's control over their own reproductive life. Women need access to late-term abortion when their health is at stake at least as much as they do to abortions earlier in their pregnancies. No third party should be allowed to interfere with the decision reached between a woman and her doctor as to which abortion procedure is best for her. Passing even one restriction strengthens the idea that women shouldn't be allowed to make this decision by themselves, even though they must live with the consequences of an unwanted or dangerous pregnancy.

Elizabeth Schulte, *International Socialist Review*, June/July 2000.

In the deprived nations of Africa, Asia and South America, word has gotten around. In the majority of cases, whenever someone appears at the doors of an emergency room with some sort of infection from a botched abortion done in a back alley shop, she is denied treatment that would be life saving, out of fear that the hospital service will be marked and denied USAID funding. "Don't touch abortion" becomes the rule of the day. More wooden boxes.

The belief seems to be that in the Third World as well as here, denying proper health care for the poor will "make them more responsible" and "motivate" them to seek out proper birth-control methods. This is just more cruel thinking. We keep trying failed policies over and over again. Statistics speak for themselves. Worldwide, a septic abortion kills a woman every two minutes. That only means more and more wooden boxes.

Choice Is the Issue

Abortion policy from the right is but a microcosm of what is the state of health care services offered to the poor women of the world today. Here in the U.S. the Pentagon spends more in fifteen minutes than is allocated for women's health care programs in a year. Progressives in the pro-choice movement are trying to get out that message. It is just this year (1999) that research centers in the U.S. have been given the go ahead to evaluate RU-486, the French self-administered oral abortion medication, already widely accepted in Europe [RU-486 was approved in the United States in September 2000 for use in early nonsurgical abortions.]. This should not be looked upon as a panacea and the need for surgical terminations will remain. But RU-486 will be a valuable addition to the methods that will give doctors and their patients those alternatives when needed. Each will have its place. It all filters down to the basics—abortion is not the issue, choice is.

The women of America need support, not only for their choice to end an unwanted pregnancy, but for prenatal care, mammographies, PAP tests, and physicians' help when needed. Health care is not a privilege. It is a right.

She was young, unmarried, pregnant, alone, and desperate. She ended up in my emergency room, bleeding, in shock, in a coma, and then dead. I've seen it before. I don't want to see it again.

It doesn't have to be that way. If we can learn to see the abortion issue clearly—not ethics but rights, not religion but science, not sexism but equality for women—we can begin to work on the dilemma.

> *"When a bystander can see a baby flinching at the moment of intentional killing, there is no 'too close [to infanticide]' about it. It is infanticide."*

Late-Term Abortions Should Be Banned

John Leo

In June 2000 the U.S. Supreme Court struck down a Nebraska ban on late-term abortions—procedures that are performed after twenty-four weeks of pregnancy and are also referred to as "partial-birth" abortions. Syndicated columnist John Leo denounces this court decision in the following viewpoint, arguing that late-term abortions are a form of legalized infanticide to which the majority of Americans strongly object. Because partial-birth abortions are always optional and are never necessary to save the life or future health of the mother, they should be outlawed, asserts Leo.

As you read, consider the following questions:

1. How does Brenda Shafer, quoted by Leo, describe the late-term abortion she witnessed?
2. In the author's opinion, what has been the effect of the Supreme Court's 1992 *Casey* decision?
3. According to Leo, how do so-called "health exceptions" undermine states' attempts to regulate abortion?

Reprinted from "Partial-Sense Decision," by John Leo, *U.S. News & World Report*, July 10, 2000. Copyright 2000, U.S. News & World Report. Visit www.usnews.com for additional information.

"**C**hampagne and shivers," abortion lobbyist Janet Benshoof said in reaction to the Supreme Court's 5-4 vote to strike down Nebraska's ban on "partial-birth" abortion. "Shivers" because the vote was close, "champagne" because the few rogue abortionists who perform this procedure can keep at it, no matter what 30 state legislatures and two thirds of the American people think.

Just to remind you what the champagne is celebrating, here is an account by Brenda Shafer, a pro-choice nurse who attended a partial-birth abortion in Ohio in 1993: "The doctor delivered the baby's legs and arms, everything but his little head. The baby's body was moving, his little fingers were clasped together. He was kicking his feet. The doctor took a pair of scissors and inserted them into the back of the baby's head and the baby's arms jerked out in a flinch, a startled reaction, like a baby does when he thinks that he might fall. Then the doctor opened the scissors up. Then he stuck a high-powered suction tube into the hole and sucked the baby's brains out." "I still have nightmares about what I saw," she added. Yes, that would seem to be an appropriate reaction.

Sen. Daniel Patrick Moynihan thinks partial-birth abortion is "too close to infanticide." I would say that when a bystander can see a baby flinching at the moment of intentional killing, there is no "too close" about it. It *is* infanticide. And with a lot of tortured mental gymnastics, it has just been protected by our highest court.

Broad Versus Narrow

The court ruled that the language of Nebraska's ban was too broad, because it seemed to ban other forms of abortion. Writing for the majority, Justice Stephen Breyer insisted that he lacked the power to interpret the law narrowly. But Justice Antonin Scalia was quick to point out that the court has often done so and was now abandoning "the principle that even ambiguous statutes should be interpreted in such fashion as to render them valid rather than void."

Breyer wrote his opinion in the distancing language favored by people who are about to approve some repugnant act: "transcervical procedures," "osmotic dilators," "instrumental disarticulation," all of it written from the technical point of view of the professional abortionist with a tough job to do. The public's clear moral revulsion seemed to go right past Breyer.

In the high court's 1992 *Casey* [*v. Planned Parenthood*] decision, the justices strongly acknowledged that the states have legitimate and important constitutional interests to assert on abortion. In effect, they shifted some decision-making power from the woman and her physician to the state.

An Extremely Painful Experience

I am [a brain surgeon,] not an obstetrician. But as I view and understand this particular abortive procedure, the partial-birth abortion—with its tissue compression, its pulling of limbs and body, its anatomical distortion—must be an extremely painful experience for the fetus as it is advanced into and through the birth canal. But what is most disturbing for me is the surgical procedure itself. Here we are talking about a brain operation on a living human fetus who has reached an age at which, if it were outside the womb, it would be a candidate for neurosurgery.

We operate on preemies within this age range, conducting brain surgery to save their lives. We would never consider any procedure giving us surgical access to a preemie's central nervous system without sophisticated neuroanesthesia to eliminate pain.

Robert J. White, *America*, October 18, 1997.

It now appears that *Casey* was a bait-and-switch effort. To placate people who expected *Roe v. Wade* to be overturned, the court said it would allow limits on abortion, but after this decision, we know it has no intention of allowing any important dent in the country's abortion machine. Justice Anthony M. Kennedy wrote a pained dissent implying that he has been double-crossed after signing on with the *Casey* majority. He also said clearly what many think of this court: It has gotten in the habit of replacing the decisions of voters and legislatures with its own personal opinions. Kennedy wrote: "The issue is not whether members of the judiciary can see a difference between [partial-birth and other procedures]. It is whether Nebraska can. The court's refusal to recognize Nebraska's right to declare a moral difference between the procedures is a dispiriting disclosure of the illogic and illegitimacy of the court's approach to the entire case."

The "Health Exceptions" Tactic

Perhaps the shabbiest of the court's tactics was to announce that a partial-birth ban must contain an exception for the health of the mother. This was unexpected, and was apparently inserted to ward off future attempts to construct a valid ban. First, the partial-birth procedure is entirely elective and is never used to save a mother's life. Many obstetricians and gynecologists, plus former Surgeon General C. Everett Koop, signed a statement pointing out that "partial-birth abortion is never medically necessary to protect a mother's health or her future fertility."

Second, the Nebraska Legislature would have had to be exceedingly stupid to insert a health exception in light of what the court said in 1973's *Doe v. Bolton*: that the health of the mother must be construed to include emotional, psychological, familial, and other factors "relevant to the well-being of the patient." In other words, health is defined so broadly and subjectively that any ban that includes a health exception would forbid no partial-birth abortions at all. Yet the court, with a straight face, insists on an exception that would seem to gut any bill that contained it. This decision appears to undermine much of the leeway given to the states in *Casey*. It seems to offer every woman and her doctor a trump card to play against the states. Justice Clarence Thomas wrote: "The majority's insistence on a health exception is a fig leaf barely covering its hostility to any abortion regulation by the states—a hostility that Casey purported to reject."

This decision shows that we don't need a better law. We need a better court.

*"'Partial-birth' abortion . . . is designed
primarily to be used in the case of 5- and
6-month-old fetuses that are dying,
malformed, or threaten the woman's
health or life."*

Late-Term Abortions Should
Not Be Banned

Glenn Woiceshyn

Late-term abortions, sometimes referred to as "partial-birth"
abortions, should not be banned, maintains Glenn Woiceshyn
in the following viewpoint. Such procedures, which are relatively rare, are essential when a woman's life or health are
threatened by her pregnancy or when a fetus has serious
physical defects, the author explains. Moreover, he asserts,
the attempt to criminalize late-term abortions is at heart an
attempt to outlaw all abortions. Woiceshyn, who wrote this
viewpoint two months before a Nebraska ban on late-term
abortions was declared unconstitutional, is a home-school
teacher and a senior writer for the Ayn Rand Institute.

As you read, consider the following questions:
1. What happens during an intact dilation and extraction
   (D&X) procedure, according to Woiceshyn?
2. According to the author, why do anti-abortionists use the
   term "partial birth" to describe late-term abortions?
3. In Woiceshyn's opinion, when do an infant's individual
   rights begin?

Reprinted from "Supreme Court Should Protect Right to Abortion in Current
Partial-Birth Case," by Glenn Woiceshyn, 2000, found at http://aynrand.org/
medialink/partial.shtml.

Anti-abortionists are making a comeback. A woman's right to abortion is rapidly being eroded by the proliferation of state laws banning certain types of abortions. On April 25, 2000, in a case known as *Carhart v. Stenberg* (No. 99-830), the Supreme Court will consider the constitutionality of one such law: Nebraska's law banning so-called "partial-birth" abortions. [In June 2000, the court declared this ban unconstitutional.]

When abortion was illegal in America, many women died or suffered serious medical problems from either self-induced or illegal "back-alley" abortions. Women streamed into emergency rooms with punctured wombs, massive bleeding, and rampant infections.

Thanks to the *Roe v. Wade* (1973) Supreme Court decision, women today have access to safe abortions by medically trained professionals under sanitary conditions. But anti-abortionists—so-called "pro-lifers"—are changing all this.

A Dangerous Precedent

State laws banning "partial-birth" abortions establish a precedent for criminalizing other types of abortion—as America slides down the bloody slope to "back-alley" abortions.

Those who are truly pro-life must grasp the ominous implications of and underlying motives behind such anti-abortion laws—before it's too late.

"Partial-birth" abortion, most commonly known as intact dilation and extraction (D&X), is designed primarily to be used in the case of 5- and 6-month-old fetuses that are dying, malformed, or threaten the woman's health or life. The procedure involves pulling the fetus from the womb, except for the head which is too large to pass without injuring the woman. The head is then collapsed to allow removal. This procedure is designed for the maximum protection of the woman. The late-term alternative to D&X, one that doesn't require partial removal, involves dismembering the fetus in the womb before extraction—a much riskier procedure.

Anti-abortionists coined the term "partial birth" to suggest that the partially removed fetus is no longer "unborn," and, therefore, *Roe v. Wade* no longer applies (so they allege). But linguistic manipulation can't create an essential distinction when none exists. A woman has a right to her own body, and, if she chooses to abort, then all effort should be made to protect the woman from injury. To rule otherwise is to negate this right.

A Perversion of Individual Rights

Banning any type of abortion to "protect the fetus" necessarily grants rights to the fetus—an utter perversion of individual rights. If a woman has no right to her own body, then by what logic does a fetus (which, by definition, is a biological parasite) have a right to the woman's body? Properly, an infant's rights begin after the fetus is removed from the mother's body and its umbilical cord cut.

It is a woman's individual rights—to her life, to her liberty, and to the pursuit of her happiness—that sanctions her right to have an abortion. Once "fetal rights" are granted to one stage of the pregnancy, nothing will prevent their extension to all stages. "Fetal rights" are a gimmick to destroy a woman's individual rights.

Tragically, many "pro-choicers" have conceded the "partial-birth" debate to the anti-abortionists and accept a ban as a compromise (and merely quibble about its scope). Such "pro-choicers" have apparently been hoodwinked by the anti-abortionists' strategy of emotionalism and evasion designed to disguise their deeper purpose.

The anti-abortionists' strategy involves focusing solely on the fetus and describing the abortion in gruesome detail. Their professed compassion for the fetus apparently leaves no room for considering the woman's health and happiness. For them, waving a picture of a bloody, mangled fetus constitutes an argument. If so, then so does waving a picture of a woman whose future was ruined because she was denied an abortion—or of a woman bloody and mangled by a "back-alley" abortion.

A picture is not an argument—and should not be allowed as a cover-up.

An Attempt to Ban All Abortions

While anti-abortionists' attacks are primarily focused on rarely performed late-term abortions, they zealously want all abortions banned. Helen Alvare, a spokeswoman for the

Catholic Bishops and a staunch enemy of D&X, has declared, "In a moral sense all abortions are equally awful."

Saving Women's Lives

It is compelling to review a few public cases of women whose lives would have been endangered had [late-term abortion bans] been law at the time of their pregnancies. . . .

Coreen Costello from Agoura, California. In April 1995, seven months pregnant with her third child, Coreen and her husband Jim found out that a lethal neuromuscular disease had left their much-wanted daughter unable to survive. Its body had stiffened and was frozen, wedged in a transverse position. In addition, amniotic fluid had puddled and built up to dangerous levels in Coreen's uterus. Devout Christians and opposed to abortion, the Costellos agonized for over two weeks about their decision and baptized the fetus in utero. Finally, Coreen's increasing health problems forced them to accept the advice of numerous medical experts that the intact dilation and extraction (D&X) was, indeed, the best option for Coreen's own health, and the abortion was performed. Later, in June 1996, Coreen gave birth to a healthy son.

Maureen Mary Britell from Sandwich, Massachusetts. Maureen and her husband Andrew, practicing Catholics, were expecting their second child in early 1994 when, at six months' gestation, a sonogram revealed that the fetus had anencephaly. No brain was developing, only a brain stem. Experts at the New England Medical Center in Boston confirmed that the fetus the Britells had named Dahlia would not survive. The Britells' parish priest supported their decision to induce labor and terminate the pregnancy. During the delivery, a complication arose and the placenta would not drop. The umbilical cord had to be cut, aborting the fetus while still in delivery in order to prevent serious health risks for Maureen. Dahlia had a Catholic funeral.

John M. Swomley, *Humanist*, March 13, 1998.

According to anti-abortionists' dogma, God places the soul in the womb at conception. Hence, via a leap of faith, the fertilized egg—a tiny speck of cells—is granted the status of human being. At that moment, the woman's status is demoted to that of slave and breeding mare—and her womb becomes God's property (which, in practice, means the government's property). The rights of the woman have therefore been sacrificed to the alleged rights of the fetus. According to this dogma, abortion is murder at any stage of the pregnancy (which explains why some "pro-lifers" feel morally sanctioned to kill doctors and bomb abortion clinics).

The anti-abortionists' war against "partial-birth" abortions is a smokescreen to ban all abortions. Abortion is a woman's moral right. To protect that right the Supreme Court must declare Nebraska's law prohibiting "partial-birth" abortions as unconstitutional. Furthermore, "pro-choicers" must reject compromise and fight any law prohibiting abortion on principle—the principle of individual rights—the principle upon which this pro-rights country was founded.

"It is not surprising . . . that many states have decided that a serious surgical procedure like abortion should . . . involve the child's parents, or in some cases, a judge."

Parental Consent Laws Are Necessary

Part I: Charles T. Canady; Part II: Eileen Roberts

The authors of the following two-part viewpoint contend that parental consent laws, which require the notification or consent of a girl's parents before she can have an abortion, are necessary. These authors also support the proposed Child Custody Protection Act, which would strengthen parental involvement laws by making it illegal to transport minors across state lines to evade consent laws in their own states. In Part I, Florida representative Charles T. Canady argues that parents are legally responsible for their child's health and therefore have a right to know if their daughter is planning to have an abortion. In Part II, Eileen Roberts, founder of Mothers Against Minors' Abortions, recounts the physical and emotional problems her daughter faced after obtaining an abortion that Roberts had not consented to.

As you read, consider the following questions:

1. What option is available for teens who want to have an abortion but are afraid to tell their parents, according to Canady?
2. What kinds of health problems did Roberts's daughter encounter after having an abortion, according to the author?

Part I: Reprinted from Charles T. Canady's testimony before the U.S. House Committee on the Judiciary, Subcommittee on the Constitution, May 27, 1999.
Part II: Reprinted from Eileen Roberts's testimony before the U.S. House Committee on the Judiciary, Subcommittee on the Constitution, May 27, 1999.

I

This morning [May 27, 1999], the Subcommittee on the Constitution convenes to hear testimony concerning H.R. 1218: The Child Custody Protection Act. The Child Custody Protection Act (CCPA) is designed to address the problem of people transporting minor girls across state lines to circumvent parental notification and consent laws.

Across this country, a child can't even be given an aspirin at school without her parent's permission. It is not surprising, then, that many states have decided that a serious surgical procedure like abortion should also involve the child's parents, or in some cases, a judge.

Disregard of Consent Laws

In fact, over twenty states currently enforce laws that require the consent or notification of at least one parent, or court authorization, before a minor can obtain an abortion. Yet, despite court approval of and overwhelming public support for these laws, vulnerable young girls are taken from their families to out-of-state abortion clinics in flagrant disregard of the legal protections the states have provided.

Indeed, studies conducted in various states demonstrate an unmistakable correlation between the number of girls seeking abortions out of state and the existence of parental consent and/or notification laws in the girls' home states. Moreover, in states requiring parental consent or notification, abortion counselors often circumvent the law by referring girls to out-of-state clinics which advertise in neighboring states that they do not require parental consent or a waiting period.

This scenario fosters hasty and ill-advised decisions in which confused, frightened young girls are coerced into having abortions by those who may not have the girls' best interest in mind. This is particularly disturbing given the fact that the majority of teenage pregnancies are caused by adult men who obviously have a great incentive to avoid criminal liability for their misconduct.

When parents are not involved in the abortion decisions of a child, the risks to the child's health significantly increases. Only parents have knowledge of their daughter's prior medical and psychological history, and would, for instance, be able to alert the abortionist of allergies to anesthesia and medication and provide authorization for the release of pertinent data from family physicians. When a pregnant girl is taken across state lines by a stranger for an abortion, none of these precautions can be taken. The Child Custody Protection Act will simply ensure the effectiveness of state laws designed to provide a layer of protection against these dangers to children's health and safety.

Abortion activists say taking girls out of state is the only option when the girls are afraid to tell their parents about their pregnancy, but this ignores the judicial bypass option that is available for just this type of situation. [This option allows minors seeking abortions to obtain consent from a judge if they are unable to tell their parents.]

The Need to Regulate Commerce

Congress has a persuasive interest in exercising its constitutional responsibility to regulate commerce. Should abortionists in Connecticut have the right to lure girls from Massachusetts to the Nutmeg State so that they can evade the supervision and counsel of their mothers? In Nevada there are whores who, unlike the whores in other states, perform legally. Should entrepreneurs in Utah be free to take minors across the line to learn a new profession? We have a federal law that prohibits this. Why is a different principle involved where abortion is concerned?

William F. Buckley Jr., *National Review*, August 30, 1999.

Abortion activists also like to claim that it is simply a loving aunt or grandmother who takes the girl for the secret out-of-state abortion, when their own study—conducted in 1992 by the Alan Guttmacher Institute—shows that in a majority of cases it is *not* a family member who accompanies the girl for an abortion without the knowledge of her parents.

Moreover, states are free to craft their parental notification and consent laws to provide that notification or consent of a grandmother or other close adult relative is sufficient to permit a minor to have an abortion without parental involvement, and such statutes would not be covered by CCPA.

Most states have not, however, chosen to allow grandmothers and other close relatives to act as surrogates for parents in the abortion context. If the minor's circumstances are such that parental involvement is not possible, the grandmother or other close relative is free to assist the minor in pursuing a judicial bypass procedure. Such relatives should follow the law, not take the minor out of State to circumvent the law.

In light of the widespread practice of circumventing state parental involvement laws by transporting minors across state lines, it is entirely appropriate for Congress, with its exclusive constitutional authority to regulate interstate commerce, to enact the Child Custody Protection Act. The safety of young girls and the rights of parents demand no less.

II

My name is Eileen Roberts. I am the founder of an organization called MAMA, which stands for Mothers Against Minors' Abortions. This organization was formed to serve as a collective voice for others also seeking to restore the rights of parents to be involved when their minor aged daughter seeks an abortion, whether in their community or for those who are taken across state lines without their knowledge or consent.

More significant, however, is the fact that I am the mother of a daughter who at age 14 underwent an abortion without my knowledge.

At age 13, the close relationship I had with my daughter was interrupted by a period of her rebelling, which included a relationship with a boy, which I knew was not in her best interest. My daughter refused my request not to see him but I continued to unconditionally love and care for her to the best of my ability, through this difficult time.

During my daughter's rebellion towards our parental authority, my daughter was encouraged by her boyfriend, with the assistance of an adult friend, to obtain a secret abortion without my knowledge. This adult friend drove my daughter to the abortion clinic, 45 miles away from our home and even paid for my daughter's abortion.

Wondering why my daughter had become depressed over the next two weeks, my husband and I thought perhaps her boyfriend had introduced her to drugs, so we searched for answers. Words cannot adequately communicate the Orwellian nightmare of discovering that your child had undergone an abortion, from a questionnaire we found under her pillow, which she failed to return to the abortion clinic.

As a result of her depression, my daughter was hospitalized, at which time it was discovered that the abortion had been incompletely performed and required surgery to repair the damage done by the abortionist. I was called and was told that my daughter could not have this reparative surgery without a signed consent form.

The following year my daughter developed an infection and was diagnosed as having pelvic inflammatory disease, which again required a two day hospitalization for IV antibiotic therapy and requiring a signed consent form.

To add insult to injury, my husband and I were responsible for our daughter's medical costs which amounted to over $27,000.

Why People Evade Consent Laws

I am here today to ask this [congressional] committee to reject the eccentric notion that any adult stranger has the right to abduct our minor aged daughters and take them to another state for a secret abortion. I speak today for those parents I know around the country, whose daughters have been taken out of state for their abortions. Many times these attempts to evade parental notification and consent laws are also attempts to conceal criminal activity, such as statutory rape. Certainly if a child is raped, a parent should know about it so this criminal can be prosecuted to the fullest extent of the law.

I am horrified that our daughters are being dumped on our driveways after they are seized from our care, made to skip school, lie, and deceive their parents to be transported across state lines, whether it be two miles or 100 miles away. Where are these strangers when the emotional and physical repercussions occur? They are driving away to once again seize and transport other teens for secret abortions, and thus the malicious activity occurs again and again. Besides, strangers are not responsible for the financial or emotional costs that occur with secret abortions—parents are.

I am reminded of the child from New York whose parents were notified in time to make funeral arrangements. Mrs. Ruth Ravenella shared with me and The Senate Education and Health Committee in Richmond, Virginia, that she sat in the hospital for three weeks before her daughter died with her hand over her mouth to help keep herself from screaming.

Restoring Family Dignity

I am aware and concerned for the many teens who are truly from abusive homes, who are snatched away, given a secret abortion and then sent back to the abuser. This activity *is* contrary to the laws of this country. These girls need to be removed from such an abusive environment and the family encouraged to seek professional counseling.

Please allow parents the opportunity to put their arms around their daughters and say, "I love you, we can work this through together," which parental notification and consent laws restore and this legislation will protect.

In conclusion, what has happened to my family, has happened that cannot be changed, however, by supporting and passing the "Child Custody Protection Act," parental notification and consent laws will be secured and I can say with confidence that our young adolescent daughters will be protected and family dignity will be restored.

"*Minors may be driven to desperate measures to maintain the confidentiality of their pregnancies.*"

Parental Consent Laws Are Harmful

Jonathan D. Klein

Many states have laws that require teenagers seeking abortions to notify their parents of their decision or to obtain their consent. In 1999, the Child Custody Protection Act was proposed as a measure that would strengthen such parental consent laws. This measure would punish people who transport girls across state lines in order to avoid consent laws in their home state. In the following viewpoint, pediatrician Jonathan D. Klein argues that such a law would severely limit teen access to safe and confidential abortions. While teens should be encouraged to discuss an abortion decision with their parents, some girls face rejection or abuse if their parents learn about their pregnancies. The possibility of parental disapproval also increases the risk that teens will resort to dangerous methods of terminating their pregnancies, Klein maintains.

As you read, consider the following questions:
1. Why do young people delay seeking help over sensitive health-care issues, according to Klein?
2. According to a survey conducted by the American Medical Association, what percentage of physicians favor confidential treatment for adolescents?

Excerpted from Jonathan D. Klein's testimony before the U.S. House Committee on the Judiciary, Subcommittee on the Constitution, May 27, 1999.

I am Dr. Jonathan Klein, a practicing pediatrician who has taken care of adolescents for the past 15 years. I am also an associate professor in the Department of Pediatrics at the University of Rochester School of Medicine. In the 15 years that I have engaged in the health care of adolescents, I have been involved with their families, extended families and other caregivers. I have taken care of adolescents in clinical settings and in institutional settings. Within organized medicine and other social service organizations, I have served on numerous national, regional and local advisory and professional committees on many issues regarding adolescent health and conferred with many colleagues across the nation on these very tough issues.

I am speaking today on behalf of the American Academy of Pediatrics, an organization representing 55,000 pediatricians throughout the nation. In addition, I am representing the Society for Adolescent Medicine, an organization of over 1,500 physicians, nurses, psychologists, social workers, nutritionists and others involved in service delivery, teaching or research on the welfare of adolescents and Advocates for Youth, a national non-profit organization dedicated to helping young people make informed and responsible decisions about their sexual and reproductive health. It provides information, training, and advocacy to youth serving organizations, policy makers and the media in the US and internationally.

It is from these perspectives and perhaps most importantly as a parent that I am here today to express our concerns about the pending legislation, H.R. 1218, the "Child Custody Protection Act." [As of December 2000, this act had not passed.] I would like to thank the Committee for this opportunity to present this statement as Congress continues to debate this issue of significance to adolescent health care.

The Importance of Communication

The American Academy of Pediatrics firmly believes that parents should be involved in and responsible for assuring medical care for our children. Moreover, we would agree that as parents we ordinarily act in the best interests of our children and that minors benefit from our advice and the emotional support we provide as parents. We strongly encourage and hope that adolescents communicate with and involve their parents or other trusted adults in important health care decisions affecting their lives. This includes those regarding pregnancy and pregnancy termination. We know and research confirms that most adolescents do so voluntarily. This is predicated not by laws but on the quality of their relationships. By its very nature family communication *is* a family responsibility. Adolescents who live in warm, loving, caring environments, who feel supported by their parents and their parents with them, will in most instances communicate with their parents in a crisis including the disclosure of a pregnancy.

My role as a pediatrician is to support, encourage, strengthen and enhance parental communication and involvement in adolescent decisions without compromising the ethics and integrity of my relationship with adolescent patients.

The stated intent by those who support mandatory parental consent laws is that it enhances family communication as well as parental involvement and responsibility. However, the evidence does not support that these laws have that desired effect. To the contrary, there is evidence that these laws may have an adverse impact on some families and that it increases the risk of medical and psychological harm to adolescents. According to the American Academy of Pediatrics, "[i]nvoluntary parental notification can precipitate a family crisis characterized by severe parental anger and rejection of the minor and her partner. One third of minors who do not inform parents already have experienced family violence and fear it will recur. Research on abusive and dysfunctional families shows that violence is at its worse during a family member's pregnancy and during the adolescence of the family's children."

Confidentiality of Care

I would like to turn my attention to the issue of confidentiality—whether adolescents can access health care services without parental consent. The American Academy of Pediatrics, and other medical and public health groups firmly believe that young people must have access to confidential health care services—including reproductive health care and abortion services. Every one of our states' laws also provide confidential access to some services for young people, whether for child abuse, STDs, drug addiction or reproductive health care. Concern about confidentiality is one of the primary reasons young people delay seeking health services for sensitive issues, whether for an unintended pregnancy or for other reasons. While parental involvement is very desirable, and should be encouraged, it may not always be feasible and it should *not* be legislated. Young people must be able to receive health care expeditiously and confidentially.

Most adolescents will seek medical care with their parent or parents' knowledge. Making services contingent on parental involvement mandatory (either parental consent or notification) however, may drastically affect adolescent decision-making. Mandatory parental consent or notification reduces the likelihood that young people will seek timely treatment for sensitive health issues. In a regional survey of suburban adolescents, only 45 percent said they would seek medical care for sexually transmitted diseases, drug abuse or birth control if they were forced to notify their parents.

| Laws That Hurt Teens

Many people who support parental consent to abortion laws do so out of genuine concern for young people. But a closer look at these laws reveals that they hurt rather than help many teens.

Teens who do not seek parental guidance are often physically and emotionally abused, or victims of incest. The story of a 13-year-old from Idaho is one of the many laced with tragedy. Impregnated by her father, this sixth-grader scheduled an abortion in a neighboring state with her mother's assistance. After learning of his daughter's intention to terminate the pregnancy, he fatally shot her.

Jennifer Coburn, *San Diego Union-Tribune*, January 10, 1996.

A teen struggling with concerns over his or her sexual health may be reluctant to share these concerns with a parent for fear of embarrassment, disapproval, or possible violence. A parent or relative may even be the cause or focus of the teen's emotional or physical problems. The guarantee of confidentiality and the adolescent's awareness of this guarantee are both essential in helping adolescents to seek health care.

For these reasons, physicians strongly support adolescents' ability to access confidential health care. A national survey conducted by the American Medical Association (AMA) found that physicians favor confidentiality for adolescents. A regional survey of pediatricians showed strong backing of confidential health services for adolescents. Of the physicians surveyed, 75 percent favored confidential treatment for adolescents. Pediatricians describe confidentiality as "essential" in ensuring that patients share necessary and factual information with their health care provider. This is especially important if we are to reduce the incidence of adolescent suicide, substance abuse, sexually transmitted diseases and unintended pregnancies.

The Opinion of Health Care Organizations

Many influential health care organizations support the provision of confidential health services for adolescents; here is what they say:

The American Academy of Pediatrics. "A general policy guaranteeing confidentiality for the teenager, except in life-threatening situations, should be clearly stated to the parent and the adolescent at the initiation of the professional relationship, either verbally or in writing."

The Society for Adolescent Medicine. "The most practical reason for clinicians to grant confidentiality to adolescent patients is to facilitate accurate diagnosis and appropriate treatment. . . . If an assurance of confidentiality is not extended, this may create an obstacle to care since that adolescent may withhold information, delay entry into care, or refuse care."

The American Medical Association. "The AMA reaffirms that confidential care for adolescents is critical to improving their health. The AMA encourages physicians to involve parents in the medical care of the adolescent patient, when it would be in the best interest of the adolescent. When in the opinion of the physician, parental involvement would not be beneficial, parental consent or notification should not be a barrier to care."

The AMA also notes that, because "the need for privacy may be compelling, minors may be driven to desperate measures to maintain the confidentiality of their pregnancies. They may run away from home, obtain a "back alley" abortion, or resort to a self-induced abortion. The desire to maintain secrecy has been one of the leading reasons for illegal abortion since 1973."

American College of Physicians. "Physicians should be knowledgeable about state laws governing the rights of adolescent patients to confidentiality and the adolescent's legal right to consent to treatment. The physician must not release information without the patient's consent unless required by the law or if there is a duty to warn another."

The American Public Health Association. APHA "urges that . . . confidential health services (be) tailored to the needs of adolescents, including sexually active adolescents, adolescents considering sexual intercourse, and those seeking information, counseling, or services related to preventing, continuing or terminating a pregnancy."

Facing a Crisis Pregnancy

Of course, it is important for young people who are facing a health-related crisis to be able to turn to someone dependable, someone they trust, to help them decide what is best. Many, many times that person is a parent. Teenagers facing a crisis pregnancy should be encouraged to involve a parent, and many do so. In fact, over 75 percent of teens under age 16 involve at least one parent in their decision, even in states that do not mandate them to do so. In some populations as many as 91% of teenagers younger than 18 years voluntarily consulted a parent or "parent surrogate" about a pregnancy decision.

All too often, however, young women know that their parents would be overwhelmed, angry, distraught or disappointed if they knew about the crisis pregnancy. Fear of emotional or physical abuse, including being thrown out of the house, are among the major reasons teenagers say they are afraid to tell their parents about a pregnancy. Young women who are afraid to involve their parents very often turn to another adult in times of difficulty. One study shows that, of young women who did not involve a parent in their abortion decision, over half turned to another adult; 15 percent of these young women involved a step-parent or other adult relative. In my own practice, I have had the situation arise in which an adult female sibling or cousin has been the person the adolescent wanted me to call into the consultation based on the fear of anger and rejection from her mother.

H.R. 1218 would harm young women who are most afraid to involve their parents in an abortion decision and who most need the support of other adults in their lives. Instead of encouraging young people to involve adults whom they trust, the law would discourage such communication. The bill would have the unintentional outcome of placing a chilling effect on teenagers' ability to talk openly with adults—including family members and medical providers—because it sends a message that adults who help young people grapple with difficult decisions are criminals. This disincentive is extremely dangerous for those young people most in need of support and guidance in a difficult time when they cannot involve their parents. . . .

Troubled Teens Need Support

In conclusion, I reiterate a statement previously made by the immediate past president of the Society for Adolescent Medicine: "[C]learly the proposed bill is designed to eliminate this [abortion]option for many adolescents. Adolescents who cannot rely on one or both parents to help them through the trauma of a pregnancy and who, for legal or geographical reasons, may need to go to an adjoining state for termination, are effectively precluded from receiving help from those (such as other relative, health professional, or even the clergy) who would be there to help them. In essence, this law would put adolescents in the position of having to take care of themselves (possibly traveling long distances in the process), without supportive care during a traumatic time in their lives."

As a physician, a teacher, and most of all, as a parent, who is concerned about the quality and safety of health care for my daughter as well as for the quality and safety of health care for all adolescents in this country, I urge you to reject H.R. 1218.

Periodical Bibliography

The following articles have been selected to supplement the diverse views presented in this chapter. Addresses are provided for periodicals not indexed in the *Readers' Guide to Periodical Literature*, the *Alternative Press Index*, the *Social Sciences Index*, or the *Index to Legal Periodicals and Books*.

Amy Bach	"No Choice for Teens," *Nation*, October 11, 1999.
William F. Buckley	"Partial Democracy from the Court," *National Review*, July 31, 2000.
Gregg Easterbrook	"Abortion and Brain Waves," *New Republic*, January 31, 2000.
Gloria Feldt	"Congress Is Foiling Americans' Desire for Reproductive Choice," *USA Today*, May 1999.
Annette Fuentes	"Back to the Womb," *In These Times*, November 28, 1999.
John F. Kavanaugh	"Killing Unborn Patients," *America*, February 19, 2000.
Miranda Kennedy	"Partial Truth Abortion Coverage," *Extra!* March/April 2000.
Judith Levine	"The Dumb-Luck Club," *Index on Censorship*, February 2000.
Bob Schaffer	"27 Years of *Roe v. Wade*," *Vital Speeches of the Day*, February 15, 2000.
Elizabeth Schulte	"The New Assault on a Woman's Right to Choose," *International Socialist Review*, June/July 2000. Available from PO Box 258082, Chicago, IL 60625.
Gary Thomas	"Roe v. McCorvey," *Christianity Today*, January 12, 1998.
Michael M. Uhlmann	"A Right to a Dead Child?" *Crisis*, November 2000.

CHAPTER 3

Can Abortion Be Justified?

Chapter Preface

Natalie Murdoch was thirty-four when she and her husband, Richard Meyer, conceived their second child. During the second trimester, an amniocentesis test revealed that their unborn child had Down syndrome—a chromosomal abnormality resulting in mild to severe physical and mental disabilities. With no way to predict the extent of these handicaps, the couple made an emotionally wrenching decision to terminate the pregnancy.

According to prenatal screening expert Eva Alberman, 92 percent of women who discover they are carrying a fetus affected by Down syndrome choose to have an abortion. Most feel that they are unequipped to take on the emotional and financial strain of raising a severely disabled child. As Natalie and Richard explain, "A seriously handicapped child takes a lot from your life that you wouldn't otherwise have to give. . . . We knew that a Down child would require, at best, constant care from us, and that would take a great deal away from [our other child]."

Many abortion opponents and advocates for the disabled strongly denounce such decisions to abort deformed or handicapped fetuses. Gregg Cunningham, director of the Center for Bio-Ethical Reform, contends that "Of the 250,000 Americans currently living with Down's Syndrome, most score in the 'mild to moderate' range of mental retardation, and most can learn to read, hold jobs, and live independently. Ought they to have been executed?" In response to those who claim that they would be unable to raise a handicapped child, Cunningham counters that there is a waiting list of parents who wish to adopt seriously disabled or retarded newborns. Cunningham and many other abortion critics agree that no handicap or genetic defect ever justifies abortion.

Some pro-choice advocates grant that the decision to abort a disabled fetus is ethically questionable. Others point out, however, that some fetal defects are so severe that the mother's life would be threatened if she were to carry the pregnancy to term. The question of whether congenital defects or any other circumstances justify abortion is the subject of the following chapter.

> "Rolling back abortion rights would merely
> ease lawmakers' consciences, while many
> women, and more late-term fetuses than
> are aborted now, would die in back alleys."

Abortion Is a "Necessary Evil"

Naomi Wolf

In the following viewpoint, author and feminist critic Naomi Wolf maintains that abortion must be seen as a serious and grave medical choice that puts an end to potential human life. Moreover, she argues, pro-choice advocates should admit that the high rate of abortion in the United States illuminates some of the nation's social and moral failings. However, denying women access to legal abortion is unethical, Wolf contends, because it results in an increase in illegal abortions that endanger the lives of women as well as their unborn children. Abortion must remain a legal—even if undesirable—option; at the same time, Americans should support programs that reduce teen pregnancy and provide access to affordable contraception, prenatal care, and adoption.

As you read, consider the following questions:
1. In Wolf's opinion, how has the rhetoric of the pro-choice movement actually undermined abortion rights in the United States?
2. According to the Alan Guttmacher Institute, cited by the author, contraception decreases the likelihood of abortion by what percentage?
3. What is the Common Ground Network for Life and Choice, according to Wolf?

Reprinted, with permission, from "Pro-Choice *and* Pro-Life," by Naomi Wolf, *The New York Times*, April 3, 1997. Copyright © 1997 by The New York Times Co.

From a pro-choice point of view, things look grim. In March 1997, came accusations that abortion-rights advocates had prevaricated about how frequently "partial birth" or "intact dilation and evacuation" abortion is performed. Then the House of Representatives voted overwhelmingly to ban the procedure. The Senate may soon address the issue, but even if it fails to override President Bill Clinton's promised veto, the pro-choice movement is staring at a great symbolic defeat. [In June 2000, bans on late-term abortion were declared unconstitutional.]

This looks like a dark hour for those of us who are pro-choice. But, with a radical shift in language and philosophy, we can turn this moment into a victory for all Americans.

How? First, let us stop shying away from the facts. Pro-lifers have made the most of the "partial birth" abortion debate to dramatize the gruesome details of late-term abortions. Then they moved on to the equally unpleasant details of second-trimester abortions. Thus, pro-lifers have succeeded in making queasy many voters who once thought that they were comfortable with *Roe v. Wade*.

Ceding the Moral High Ground

Unfortunately, we set ourselves up for this. Our rhetoric has long relied on euphemism. An abortion was simply "a woman's choice." We clung to a neutral, abstract language of "privacy" and "rights." This approach was bound to cede the moral high ground to our opposition and to guarantee an erosion of support for abortion rights. Thirty percent of Americans support abortion based on the "woman's choice" argument alone, but when people are asked whether abortion should be a matter between "a woman, her doctor, her conscience and her God," 70 percent agree.

By ignoring this hunger for a moral framework around legal abortion, we inadvertently played into the drama that was performed before Congress. When someone holds up a model of a six-month-old fetus and a pair of surgical scissors, we say, "choice," and we lose.

Some pro-choicers have recently resorted to heartless medicalese to explain away the upsetting details of late abortions, pointing out that no major surgery is pretty. Such responses make us seem disconnected from our own humane sensibilities. We should acknowledge what most Americans want us to: that abortion at any stage, since it involves the possibility of another life, is a grave decision qualitatively different from medical choices that involve no one but ourselves.

What if we transformed our language to reflect the spiritual perceptions of most Americans? What if we called abortion what many believe it to be: a failure, whether that failure is of technology, social support, education, or male and female responsibility? What if we called policies that sustain, tolerate and even guarantee the highest abortion rate of any industrialized nation what they should be called: crimes against women?

A More Effective Strategy

If we frankly acknowledged abortion as a necessary evil, a more effective and ethical strategy falls into place. Instead of avoiding pictures of mangled fetuses as if they were pro-life propaganda, we could claim them as our own most eloquent testimony.

Rolling back abortion rights would merely ease lawmakers' consciences, while many women, and more late-term fetuses than are aborted now, would die in back alleys, deaths as agonizing as those that pro-lifers have been so graphically describing. No woman, we should argue, should have to make the terrible choice of a late abortion if there is any alternative. And these late abortions are more likely to occur when 80 percent of women have to travel outside of their counties to end a pregnancy.

The moral of such awful scenes is that a full-fledged campaign for cheap and easily accessible contraception is the best antidote to our shamefully high abortion rate. Use of birth control lowers the likelihood of abortion by 85 percent, according to the Alan Guttmacher Institute. More than half of unplanned pregnancies occur because no contraception was used. If we asked Americans to send checks to Planned Parenthood to help save hundreds of thousands of women a year from having to face abortions, our support would rise exponentially.

A year of sexual responsibility can easily cost someone $200 or more (and that someone is likely to be female). To those who oppose access to contraceptives, yet hold up images of dead fetuses, we should say: This disaster might have been prevented by a few cents' worth of nonoxynol-9; this blood is on your hands.

A World of Genuine Choice

Try to imagine real gender equality. Actually, try to imagine an America that is female-dominated, since a true working democracy in this country would reflect our 54-46 voting advantage.

Now imagine such a democracy, in which women would be valued so very highly, as a world that is accepting and responsible about human sexuality; in which there is no coerced sex without serious jailtime; in which there are affordable, safe contraceptives available for the taking in every public health building; in which there is economic parity for women—and basic economic subsistence for every baby born; and in which every young American woman knows about and understands her natural desire as a treasure to cherish, and responsibly, when the time is right, on her own terms, to share.

In such a world, in which the idea of gender as a barrier has become a dusty artifact, we would probably use a very different language about what would be—then—the rare and doubtless traumatic event of abortion. That language would probably call upon respect and responsibility, grief and mourning. In that world we might well describe the unborn and the never-to-be-born with the honest words of life.

And in that world, passionate feminists might well hold candlelight vigils at abortion clinics, standing shoulder to shoulder with the doctors who work there, commemorating and saying goodbye to the dead.

Naomi Wolf, *New Republic*, October 16, 1995.

For whatever the millions of pro-lifers think about birth control, abortion must surely be worse. A challenge to pro-choicers to abandon a dogmatic approach must be met with a challenge to pro-lifers to separate from the demagogues in their ranks and join us in a drive to prevent unwanted pregnancy.

The Common Ground Network

The Common Ground Network for Life and Choice has brought activists together from both sides. They are working on ensuring better prenatal care; making adoption easier; reducing the rate of teen pregnancy through programs that give girls better opportunities and offer them mentors; and rejecting violent means of protest. They have teamed abortion clinics to prenatal care and adoption clinics to give desperate women real choices. The network has even found that half of the pro-lifers in some of its groups would support a campaign to improve access to birth control.

The pro-choice movement should give God a seat at the table. For many good reasons, including the religious right's often punitive use of Scripture and the ardently anti-abortion position of the Roman Catholic Church, the pro-choice movement has been wary of God-based arguments.

But on issues of values like abortion and assisted suicide, the old Marxist-Freudian, secular-materialist left has run out of both ideas and authority. The emerging "religious left" is where we must turn for new and better ideas. We should call on the ministers, priests and rabbis of the religious left to explain their support of abortion rights in light of what they understand to be God's will.

America is a religious country—and a pluralistic one. Even in debate about "partial birth" abortion, unspoken religious assumptions and differences play a part. While Judaism generally maintains that in a choice between the fetus and the mother, the mother's life, with its adult obligations, must always come first, traditional Catholic teaching holds that you cannot directly kill a fetus to save the life of the mother. Americans must be reminded that people of faith can reach different conclusions about abortion.

Real Choice

Finally, we must press Congress to work with the Clinton Administration to take this approach to the national level. On January 22, 1997, Hillary Rodham Clinton, Vice President Al Gore and Tipper Gore took the extraordinary step of calling on abortion providers and their opponents to reject extremism, support efforts to lower the abortion rate and talk with those who do not share their views.

Now lawmakers must follow through with sweeping policies to give that sentiment substance. Congress and the Administration should champion the "common ground" approach, and add to it bipartisan support for financing far more research, development and distribution of contraceptives.

We have all lived with the human cost of our hypocrisies for too long. It is time to abandon symbolic debates on Capitol Hill in favor of policies that can give women—who have been so ill-served by the rigid views on both sides—real help and real choice.

"The rhetoric of abortion as a necessary evil is designed to sideline Americans' moral qualms about abortion."

The "Necessary Evil" Argument Does Not Justify Abortion

Clarke D. Forsythe

Clarke D. Forsythe is an attorney and the president of Americans United for Life in Chicago, Illinois. In the following viewpoint, Forsythe declares that the notion of abortion as a "necessary evil" is simply a rhetorical tactic used by activists who wish to keep abortion legal. He argues that abortion advocates have successfully spread several myths that have convinced the majority of Americans to support legalized abortion even though they generally believe it is immoral. These myths include exaggerations about the number of women who have died from botched illegal abortions, the author asserts. Such ideas have reinforced the belief that there are only two options in the abortion debate: legal abortions or dangerous back-alley abortions. Americans must be shown alternatives to these choices if they are to have an honest public dialogue on abortion, Forsythe concludes.

As you read, consider the following questions:
1. According to a Gallup study cited by Forsythe, what percentage of Americans believe that abortion is the "taking of human life?"
2. In the author's opinion, what are the four myths about abortion that have been disseminated since the 1960s?
3. What has thwarted democratic debate on the abortion issue, in Forsythe's view?

Reprinted, with permission of the author, from "Abortion Is Not a 'Necessary Evil,'" by Clarke D. Forsythe, *Christianity Today*, May 24, 1999.

M ore than twenty-six years after the Supreme Court's *Roe v. Wade* decision, the public debate on abortion seems to have reached a stalemate. The issue continues to be debated in Congress and state legislatures across the country, but, year to year, there seems to be little change in public opinion.

This does not mean, however, that the abortion issue is going to recede in intensity any time soon. There are many reasons for this, but perhaps the most important is simply that "the majority of Americans morally disapprove of the majority of abortions currently performed," as University of Virginia sociologist James Hunter concludes in his path-breaking 1994 book, *Before the Shooting Begins: Searching for Democracy in America's Culture Wars.* Hunter's analysis is based on the 1991 Gallup poll "Abortion and Moral Beliefs," the most thorough survey of American attitudes toward abortion yet conducted.

The Gallup study found that 77 percent of Americans believe that abortion is at least the "taking of human life" (28 percent), if not "murder" itself (49 percent). Other polls confirm these findings. And yet, while many Americans—perhaps 60 percent in the middle—see legalized abortion as an evil, they see it as "necessary."

The *Chicago Tribune* aptly summarized the situation in a September 1996 editorial: "Most Americans are uncomfortable with all-or-nothing policies on abortion. They generally shy away from proposals to ban it in virtually all circumstances, but neither are they inclined to make it available on demand no matter what the circumstances. They regard it, at best, as a necessary evil."

If Middle America—as Hunter calls the 60 percent—sees abortion as an evil, why is it thought to be necessary? Although the 1991 Gallup poll did not probe this question specifically, it made clear that it is not because Middle America sees abortion as necessary to secure equal opportunities for women. For example, less than 30 percent believe abortion is acceptable in the first three months of pregnancy if the pregnancy would require a teenager to drop out of school (and the number drops below 20 percent if the abortion is beyond three months). Likewise, less than 20 percent support abortion in the first three months of pregnancy if the pregnancy would interrupt a woman's career (and that support drops to 10 percent if the abortion is after the third month).

Four "Necessary" Myths

Instead, many Americans, therefore, may see abortion as "necessary" to avert "the back alley." In this sense, the notion of legal abortion as a "necessary evil" is based on a series of myths widely disseminated since the 1960s. These myths captured the public mind and have yet to be rebutted.

Myth #1: One to two million illegal abortions occurred annually before legalization. In fact, the annual total in the few years before abortion on demand was no more than tens of thousands and most likely fewer. For example, in California, the most populous state where it was alleged that 100,000 illegal abortions occurred annually in the 1960s, only 5,000 abortions were performed in 1968, the first full year of legalization.

Myth #2: Thousands of women died annually from abortions before legalization. As a leader in the legalization movement, Dr. Bernard Nathanson later wrote: "How many deaths were we talking about when abortion was illegal? In N.A.R.A.L. [National Abortion and Reproductive Rights League] we generally emphasized the drama of the individual case, not the mass statistics, but when we spoke of the latter it was always '5,000 to 10,000 deaths a year.' I confess that I knew the figures were totally false, and I suppose that others did too if they stopped to think of it. But in the 'morality' of our revolution, it was a useful figure, widely accepted, so why go out of our way to correct it with honest statistics?"

In fact, the U.S. Centers for Disease Control (CDC) statistics in 1972 show that 39 women died from illegal abortion and 27 died from legal abortion.

Myth #3: Abortion law targeted women rather than abortionists before legalization. In fact, the nearly uniform policy of the states for nearly a century before 1973 was to treat the woman as the second victim of abortion.

Myth #4: Legalized abortion has been good for women. In fact, women still die from legal abortion, and the general impact on health has had many negative consequences, including the physical and psychological toll that many women bear, the epidemic of sexually transmitted disease, the general coarsening of male-female relationships over the past 30 years, the threefold increase in the repeat-abortion rate, and the increase in hospitalizations from ectopic pregnancies.

A generation of Americans educated by these myths sees little alternative to legalized abortion. It is commonly believed that prohibitions on abortion would not reduce abortion and only push thousands of women into "the back alley" where many would be killed or injured. Prohibitions would mean no fewer abortions and more women injured or killed. Wouldn't that be worse than the status quo?

Elevating the Public Debate

Middle America's sense that abortion is a necessary evil explains a lot of things, and, by giving coherent explanation to many disparate facts and impressions, it may provide a way beyond the stalemate to—as Hunter calls for—an elevation in the content and conduct of the public debate.

First, this notion of abortion as a necessary evil explains the seemingly contradictory polls showing that a majority of Americans believe both that abortion is murder and that it should be legal. The most committed pro-life Americans see legality and morality to be inextricably intertwined and therefore view the polling data as contradictory. But Middle America understands "legal" versus "illegal" not in moral terms but in practical terms—criminalizing the procedure. Based on the historical myths, Middle America believes that criminalizing abortion would only aggravate a bad situation.

Second, the myth of abortion as a necessary evil also explains the power of the "choice" rhetoric. For the most committed abortion proponents, "choice" means moral autonomy. But there are less ideological meanings. According to the choice rhetoric, Americans can persuade women to make another choice, but they can't make abortion illegal, because that would mean no fewer abortions and simply push women into the back alley. This explains why Middle America will support virtually any regulation, short of making abortions illegal, that will encourage alternatives and reduce abortions.

In a sense, by supporting legal regulations but not prohibitions, many Americans may believe that they are choosing "the lesser of two evils."

A Pro-Abortion Tactic

The rhetoric of abortion as a "necessary evil" (though not the phrase itself) is a key tactic of abortion advocates. It is roughly reflected in President Bill Clinton's slogan that he wants abortion to be "safe, legal, and rare" and is at the heart of the President's veto of the federal partial-birth abortion bill. In the face of polls showing that 70 to 80 percent of Americans oppose the procedure, the President says that the procedure is horrible (it's an evil) but contends that "a few hundred women" every year must have the procedure (it's necessary).

The "Necessary Evil" Myth

The most enduring and effective argument that abortion proponents have used over the last 30 years can be summed up in the coat hanger. It is a practical argument, not a philosophical one. It is the reason polls show that a majority of Americans think abortion is murder, and that it should nonetheless remain legal: alternatives, prevention, adoption—yes. Criminalizing—no. (This also explains why most Americans support practically any regulations short of criminalization.)

There will be no dramatic change in public opinion until the pro-life cause does the heavy lifting that is required to overcome the myth of abortion as a necessary evil.

Clarke D. Forsythe, *National Review*, December 20, 1999.

Indeed, the rhetoric of abortion as a necessary evil is designed to sideline Americans' moral qualms about abortion. For example, when Congress first began to consider the bill prohibiting partial-birth abortion, abortion advocates bought a full-page advertisement in the *New York Times* showing a large coat hanger and the caption, "Will this be the only approved method of abortion?" The coat hanger, reinforcing the image of the back alley, remains a powerful rhetorical symbol. It reinforces the notion that there are two and only two alternatives: abortion on demand or the back alley.

Finally, the myth of abortion as a "necessary evil" also explains why 49 percent of Americans may believe that abortion is "murder" without translating this into fervent social or political mobilization. While Middle Americans may view abortion as an evil, they view it as intractable. For this reason, they view fervent campaigns to prohibit abortion as unrealistic if not counterproductive, while they are drawn to realistic alternatives and regulations. They agree that there are too many abortions and would like to see them reduced. Abortion is not a galvanizing electoral issue for Middle America, because Middle America doesn't see that much can be done about the issue legally or politically.

The Future of Abortion

The myth of abortion as a necessary evil has serious implications for future public debate. First, it means that abortion opponents have won the essential debate that the unborn is a human being and not mere tissue. In fact, the whole thrust of the "choice" argument admits this and seeks to sideline Americans' moral qualms by telling Americans that, even if it is a human life, the most that can be done is to persuade women not to have abortions.

Second, it means that the ideological arguments of both sides ("choice" versus "child") often miss the much more practical concerns of many Americans.

Third, it means that Americans balance the fate of the woman and the fate of the child. Although they understand the fate of the child to be fatal, they want to avoid the same result for women and believe that legalized abortion has been good generally for women.

This means that maximizing the fatal impact of abortion through, for example, graphic pictures of aborted babies is not a "silver bullet" that will transform public opinion alone. Instead, elevating the content and conduct of the public debate requires addressing both aspects—the impact on women as well as the impact on the child. Helping the public understand the impact on both, and the alternatives available, may contribute to a renewal of public dialogue that we so sorely need on this issue.

But a renewal of the public dialogue won't mean much if the people are not allowed to express the public will on this issue, as they usually do in our democratic republic. In 1973, the Supreme Court claimed hegemony over the issue and created a nationwide rule of abortion on demand, preventing democratic debate and solutions. The public policy dictated by the Supreme Court collides with majority opinion and reflects the views of only the 20 percent who are committed to abortion on demand. More than twenty-six years later, that is the main reason the pot keeps boiling.

"If a 14-year-old [rape victim] . . . can't have an abortion without being dragged through the courts . . . and having people trying to stop her left and right, who can?"

Rape Justifies Abortion

Margaret Sykes

In the following viewpoint, Margaret Sykes protests against commentators, political candidates, and others who opposed a second-trimester abortion for a fourteen-year-old Arizona girl who had been raped. Some anti-abortion advocates argued that the girl should not have been given federal funds to pay for her abortion; others believed that she should have birthed the child and put it up for adoption. Sykes maintains that any victim of rape should be able to easily obtain an abortion. Moreover, she contends, the attempt to control access to abortions through court-approval processes—as was the case with the Arizona rape victim—is a hypocritical tactic of anti-abortion activists. Such activists really want to outlaw all abortions, the author asserts. Sykes is a researcher and writer with a special interest in reproductive issues.

As you read, consider the following questions:
1. What is the Hyde Amendment, according to Sykes?
2. In the author's opinion, why is adoption not necessarily the best solution to an unwanted pregnancy?
3. According to Sykes, what kinds of restrictions on reproductive rights occur in U.S. hospitals?

This is an open letter to doomed [former] presidential candidate Steve Forbes, Internet pin-up girl Laura Schlessinger, and anyone else who opposed an abortion for that 14-year-old Arizona rape victim.

Please, guys. Just tell us what you want. Is that too much to ask?

I mean, if a 14-year-old girl who doesn't have a home or a family and who got pregnant when she was raped at age 13 can't have an abortion without being dragged through the courts and the newspapers and having people trying to stop her left and right, who can? Do you want every woman to wonder what might happen to *her*, if she needs an abortion that's permitted by state and federal law but might upset some fetus freak? Just tell us, okay?

Should Rape Victims Be Forced to Give Birth?

What was the problem here? Is it that this rape victim was only 14 years old? Do you want to force a girl in her early teens to become a mother after being raped, but not someone like, say, *your wife*, Mr. Forbes? Just tell us, please.

Is it that she needed public funds to pay for the abortion? But even the Hyde Amendment currently says that federal funds can be used to pay for an abortion if the pregnancy resulted from rape. Are you folks saying that this law doesn't go far enough? Do you now want to make poor women carry their rape-caused pregnancies to term, while better-off women like, say, *your wife*, Mr. Forbes, can pay to have their abortions quietly? Could you just tell us what you want?

Is it that the teen was 23 weeks pregnant? Surely that's not it. I mean, all you "pro-lifers" have told us and *told* us and *told* us that abortion is just as bad whether it takes place at 23 hours or 23 days or 23 weeks. You've opposed every piece of legislation based on the length of a woman's pregnancy because you didn't want us to get the impression that early abortions are somehow better than later ones. You say that "viability" doesn't make any difference, and that embryos and fetuses are complete human children from the second after fertilization to the second before birth. Were you *lying* about all this? Maybe late-term fetuses are a bit more like babies than speck-sized embryos after all. Can you be honest for once? Just tell us.

The raped 14-year-old first asked to have an abortion when she was 14 weeks pregnant. Would that have been okay? Do you want to add to your legislative wish list that women can only have abortions when they are raped *and* only when they are less than a certain number of weeks along? Just tell us. We need to know.

Adoption Is No Solution

"Dr. Laura," you were among those who said that both the teen and her baby "should be adopted." Well, Laura, this girl has been in foster care since she was 5, and apparently she didn't like it much. Could it be, perhaps, that she's decided not to become a mother until she knows she's ready to take care of her own child? Maybe she's not ready to risk letting *her* child be raised by someone else. Shouldn't we really be congratulating this young woman for not bringing a child into the world that she can't love and take care of, instead of shouting "Have it adopted" at her?

And isn't it funny that all the pledges of support for this girl were contingent on her giving birth? Are you going to offer to adopt her now that she's had the abortion, Laura? Are you going to adopt any of the other thousands of young girls who also don't have homes or families to love them and are at risk in exactly the same way as this girl you were beating your scrawny breast about, a day or so ago? Why is that after all the hoopla, not *one* Arizona child currently available for adoption has had someone ask to adopt any of them? Do you want children needing homes to be adopted, or do you just want to use them as fodder for your rants? Just tell us, if you can.

Mr. Forbes, you state your abortion position on your www.forbes2000.com website. After blathering on about this and that, you end with: "Steve supports a human life amendment to the Constitution, except in the cases of rape, incest and the life of the mother."

"*Except in the case of rape.*" Did you forget that when you howled, also on your website at Forbes Mourns Arizona Supreme Court Decision . . . the decision that upheld a lower-court judge's approval of the teenager's abortion . . . that "This decision is a murderous affront to decency?" Is consistency too much to expect of someone who's running for president? Please tell us.

Pro-Life Hypocrisy

Maybe you've guessed by the tone of this letter that I'm disgusted with all of you. Well, I am. I'm disgusted that the confidential details of this girl's sad situation were leaked by state officials to John Jakubczyk, the president of Arizona Right to Life. I hope the culprits are discovered and punished, but they probably won't be.

© Ann Telnaes. Used with permission.

I'm disgusted at the relatives who are suddenly coming out of the woodwork, each one claiming that they really care about the girl and want to give her a home. They sure sound like they know what she needs. "She has no choice but to behave around me or I'll whup on her butt or set her in her room," says her uncle Bob Harkins. Funny, the way she kept running away from him.

I'm disgusted at the hypocrisy and muddled thinking displayed by "pro-lifers" who on the one hand want to have teenagers go to judges to get permission for abortions if they can't tell their parents, yet call for judges who give permission for abortions judicial activists who ought to be removed from the bench.

I'm disgusted that "pro-lifers" want to pass laws restricting my right to get an abortion, yet don't want to live by those same laws once they are passed.

I'm disgusted that nobody who opposed this particular abortion will be honest about the reasons why.

Steve and Laura and the rest of you, I'm disgusted, all right. You're talking out of both sides of your mouth. If what you really want is that no woman should ever be secure in thinking that she can have an abortion if she needs or wants one, then please just say so. Don't let us be lulled into a false sense of security because of what the laws say, if you're going to oppose even lawful abortions on some unstated, unpredictable basis.

Restrictions on Reproductive Rights

Most American women probably don't know that you've already seen to it they won't get treatment to prevent pregnancy in hospitals after they are raped.

They probably don't know that heart patient Michelle Lee was turned down for an abortion when her doctors couldn't prove she was more than 50% likely to die if she continued her pregnancy, because hospital officials were afraid to interpret the laws you've passed more favorably to Michelle.

They probably don't know that another woman's abortion was turned down when her membranes ruptured at 14 weeks, making it impossible to save either the pregnancy or the fetus and necessitating an emergency abortion to save *her* from the risk of infection, because you've let Catholic hospitals get away with imposing their religious values on everyone else.

Most American women don't know that their ability to obtain an abortion—even if they've been raped or need the abortion for health reasons—has already been restricted.

If you're hoping to restrict our access to abortion even more, please tell us. We want to know, because it's going to affect things like how we vote in the next election.

Just tell us what you want our access to abortion to look like. Just tell us when we can expect our own medical care to be taken over by the Catholic Church, or by some hospital committee interpreting your laws, or by government officials sneaking our private information to the local fetus freak. Is that too much to ask?

| *"Abortion does absolutely nothing to help women and girls who have been raped or suffered incestuous sexual assault."*

Rape Does Not Justify Abortion

William Norman Grigg

Sexual assault does not justify abortion, contends William Norman Grigg in the following viewpoint. Abortion only creates more trauma for victims of rape and incest—especially in cases involving teenage victims, who often develop strong feelings of attachment to their unborn children, reports Grigg. Moreover, he argues, all human life is sacred; the means by which a child is conceived should have no bearing on the worth of that child's life. As support for his argument, Grigg discusses the case of Lee Ezell, a woman who became pregnant by rape as a teenager and gave the child up for adoption. This adoptee, who eventually became acquainted with her birth mother, now works on behalf of pregnant rape victims and their unborn children. Grigg is a senior editor for *New American*, a biweekly journal published by the John Birch Society.

As you read, consider the following questions:

1. According to Julie Makimaa, quoted by the author, how does the pro-abortion movement depict children of rape and incest?
2. In what way do Planned Parenthood counselors discourage pregnant girls from giving their children up for adoption, according to Grigg and Makimaa?
3. According to this viewpoint, how many unborn children have been destroyed by abortion?

Excerpted from William Norman Grigg, "The 'Unwanted' Child," *The New American*, January 17, 2000. Reprinted with permission.

According to a familiar legal axiom, hard cases make bad law. Abortion proponents have long capitalized upon the propaganda value of hard cases, such as pregnancies that result from rape and incest. By filtering the subject of abortion through the distorting lens of such situations, supporters of abortion on demand have exploited the sympathy of decent people to advance the notion that a child's right to life is contingent upon the circumstances of his conception. However, as Dr. Charles Rice of the University of Notre Dame Law School observes, to allow for abortions in the "hard cases" is to say "that the question of which babies will be killed is negotiable." Julie Makimaa is alive today because her mother, who became pregnant with Julie as a result of rape, understood that her child was a non-negotiable blessing.

"It doesn't matter how I began," explains Julie, who lives with her husband Bob and two teenage children in western Michigan. "What matters is who I will become." Julie is the founder of Fortress International, which works on behalf of women who become pregnant through sexual assault and the children thus conceived. She has offered testimony to Congress, as well as state legislatures in Louisiana, South Carolina, Missouri, and Tennessee. Pro-life leaders in Ireland sought out Julie's help during that nation's debate over legalizing abortion. Julie has spoken before school, civic, church, and youth groups across the country, and appeared on numerous radio and television programs. Hers is an eloquent and compelling voice offering a message of hope in the context of the tragedy of sexual assault.

Each Child Is a Miracle

"One of the truly perverse things that the pro-abortion movement has done is to convince many people that the child conceived in rape can never have a worthwhile life," Julie maintains. "The pro-abortion movement constantly depicts children of rape and incest as somehow defective, tainted, unwanted—almost as if we carry some evil gene predisposing us to anti-social behavior. While Christians certainly understand the reality of man's sinful nature, we should also understand, as my birth mother did, that each child is a God-made miracle, and that this is true of children conceived in rape and incest."

Julie has collaborated with Dave Reardon, author of the study *Aborted Women: Silent No More*, on a forthcoming book examining the "hard cases" of rape and incest. Drawing from the experiences of 264 women and children, the new study documents that "abortion does absolutely nothing to help women and girls who have been raped or suffered incestuous sexual assault," she explains. "It is another violent act that compounds the problem. In spite of the fact that killing the child may offer a quick short-term solution, it does very serious long-term damage to the girl, as millions of women are now tragically learning."

This damage is particularly pronounced in teenage victims of rape and incest who are lured into aborting their children. "Counselors for Planned Parenthood excel in preying upon the fears of troubled young girls who consider giving their children up for adoption," Julie explains. "One of the favorite approaches used by Planned Parenthood counselors is to tell young girls, 'Oh, there's no one who could love your child the way that you do' and then insist that somehow killing the child is a more compassionate alternative" than giving the baby up for adoption. Another favorite tactic, Julie continues, is to insist that "'we can't force these young girls to have babies.' But people who recite that line refuse to address the fact that having teenagers *kill* their babies is much more traumatic. What we have found in our studies is that the younger the girls, the more attached they have become to their child. When they are pressured into having an abortion, their sense of vulnerability compounds the trauma; their sense of helplessness is magnified by their inability to protect their child."

Shattered Dreams

Julie's birth mother, Lee Ezell, was a teenager who became pregnant as the result of rape. The daughter of an abusive, alcoholic father, Lee fled Philadelphia for California in 1962. As a devout Christian she anticipated falling in love, raising a family, and living a "Doris Day life" with the man for whom she was saving herself. But Lee's hopes received a brutal setback when an acquaintance at work, acting with pre-meditated malice, contrived a situation in which he could force himself upon her. The vile assault left the teenager wounded, confused, and pregnant. Compounding her problems was the fact that her alcoholic mother, who had also fled to California, reacted to Lee's news by throwing her out of their home, telling her to "take care of it" and to "come back when it's over." Homeless, jobless, with only a few dollars in savings, Lee was "an unwanted child pregnant with an unwanted child," she recalls in her book *The Missing Piece*.

Abortion Is No Solution to Rape

Why do some people believe abortion can be justified in the case of rape? Some people believe in good faith that when rape results in pregnancy, abortion can remove the painful evidence of that rape. But will it?

Will abortion erase the memory of the rape or heal the emotional and physical pain of the assault? Will abortion, in effect, erase the rape of a woman? Hardly. Rape is an act of violence inflicted upon a woman. She is an innocent victim, and this knowledge may someday help her to come to terms with the rape and rebuild her life. Abortion, on the other hand, is an act of violence that a mother inflicts on her own child. Through abortion, the mother becomes the aggressor, and this knowledge may haunt her long after she has dealt with the rape.

American Life League pamphlet, 1995.

Although the *Roe v. Wade* decision was years away, some of Lee's friends were aware of women who had solved their "problems" by undergoing illegal abortion; this was probably what her mother had alluded to when she told Lee to "take care of" her child. One of her friends suggested that she repair to an abortuary in Mexico to "get rid of this thing I didn't deserve." But Lee knew that this would be wrong. "It seemed abortion was such a permanent solution to a temporary problem," writes Lee. "I knew enough to know that one of God's commandments was 'Thou Shalt Not Kill.' If I was really serious about letting God run my life, then this wasn't an option." Through her older sister's intervention, Lee was able to arrange new living quarters with a relative. By immersing herself in prayer and Bible study, she was able to receive the strength and solace necessary to confront what seemed like an almost insurmountable challenge.

With God's help, Lee was able to forgive those who had offended her, including her parents and her assailant. With the help of a supportive congregation in Los Angeles, she was drawn more deeply into Christian fellowship. "Given my lack of spiritual maturity, I don't know what choice I would have made if abortion was as easily accessible then as it is today," Lee reflects. "Yes, there had been an illegitimate and illegal act. But the life inside me was now in the hands of God, and there were no illegitimate births when it was God who created life."

Although men may commit rape and other hideous crimes, Lee observes, "it's God who decides when to make life." Lee later discovered that Ethel Waters, a black gospel singer who was featured at the Billy Graham crusade where Lee pledged her life to Christ, "was the result of her twelve-year-old mother being raped at knife-point in a parking lot. . . . Her mother didn't volunteer for her, just as I didn't volunteer for Julie. Both Ethel and Julie were God's ideas—and He's the One who gives us worth."

New Beginnings

Lee was placed under anesthesia when she gave birth to Julie, and was never able to hold or even to see her child. "After the birth, I was passed papers to sign and told only, 'You had a healthy baby girl,'" she recounts. "I never got to see her. . . . I knew the adoption records were sealed, and that I'd never know whether the county [adoption agency] placed her with a Christian couple, as I'd requested." With the help of her Christian singles' group, Lee graduated from Bible college. She became active in organizing Bible conferences and began to write and speak about challenges facing Christian women.

In 1973 Lee met Harold Ezell, whose life had also been touched by tragedy: His first wife had died from cancer, his second wife from a rare blood disease. Lee and Harold were married six months later. Although they could have no children together, Lee developed a loving relationship with

Harold's daughters, Pam and Sandi, and was blessed with an example of what she calls "God's irony": "I sat in the same adoption courtroom where Julie's parents had adopted her and adopted Hal's girls, Pam and Sandi, as my own! I had given up a precious child for adoption, and God gave me two children to mother. I knew that if God could work things out for me, surely he would work things out for the child I'd given up."

Julie had found her way into the home of a loving Christian couple, Harold and Eileen Anderson, and learned at age seven that she was an adopted child. Although the news unsettled her, her adoptive mother explained that "it was out of love that my birth mother allowed me to have a home and parents—something she couldn't provide for me." "I often wondered who my birth mother was and if I looked like her," Julie continues. "And I never stopped hoping that she, too, was a Christian."

Julie Finds Her Birth Mother

In 1984, as a new mother, Julie contacted the Adoptees' Liberty Movement Association (ALMA), a volunteer organization that helps adopted children search out their birthmothers. ALMA placed Julie in touch with the Christian family who had provided a home for Lee while she was pregnant. On December 2nd of that year, Lee called Julie, the child she had given up two decades earlier. "Because I thought this might be our only conversation, I was careful not to ask much or make her uncomfortable," Julie relates. "I told her I had two motivations for trying to find her: to let her know she was a grandmother, and to tell her what Christ had done in my life."

By this time, Lee had become a best-selling Christian author, syndicated radio host, and highly sought-after motivational speaker, and her husband Hal was the Western Commissioner of the Immigration and Naturalization Service. When Julie and her family flew to Washington, D.C., to meet her birth mother, her husband Bob drew Lee aside and told her, "I would like to thank you for not aborting Julie. That might have been the most convenient thing to do. I just can't imagine living my life without her—or without my baby." Lee writes: "I was so grateful no 'free clinic' had been available to tempt me those many years ago."

Defeating the Death Culture

Every Mother's Day, Julie observes, she thanks "both my mothers, one who gave me the priceless gift of life, and the other who gave me the irreplaceable gift of years of love and teaching." Through Fortress International, she has learned that "those who gave up a child for adoption say that despite the emotional pain, they know they gave that child the best hope for a good life. But those who aborted babies now plead with pregnant women not to believe the lies that the 'fetus' really isn't a baby, or that abortion and its aftereffects are painless."

The abortion culture "is entirely built upon lies and deception," Julie emphasizes. "Those lies have destroyed nearly 40 million pre-born children, and have disfigured the lives of tens of millions more. Three decades after *Roe v. Wade*, we have to confront the fact that abortion has affected the lives of nearly all of us. It's very rare to find an American family that has not felt the impact of abortion in some way. So there's a real challenge confronting those of us who seek to restore respect for life. We have to be willing, first of all, to reach out in unconditional love to women who are either considering abortion or who have made the mistake of allowing their child to be killed by an abortionist. To defeat the culture of death, we must confront it with God's love."

> *"I am forever thankful for the legal choice to end the life of a baby that I believed had no chance."*

Congenital Defects May Justify Abortion

Jenny Deam

In the following viewpoint, journalist Jenny Deam discusses how she and her husband arrived at the decision to terminate their pregnancy after discovering that the fetus had a rare and often fatal birth defect. The couple was initially determined to have this child in spite of the difficulties such a birth would entail. However, by the fourth month of pregnancy, the fetus had developed such serious medical complications that the chances for its survival plummeted. Deam grieved the loss of her baby, but she feels that she made the right choice. She concludes that the decision to end a pregnancy is much more complex than those on either side of the abortion issue make it out to be.

As you read, consider the following questions:

1. According to Deam, what percentage of abortions are performed on women who are more than halfway through their pregnancies?
2. How did living in Florida affect the Deams' decision to terminate their pregnancy?
3. Why is the author angry at those on both sides of the abortion debate?

Reprinted, with permission, from Jenny Deam, "Losing Daniel," *Ladies' Home Journal*, November 1998. Originally appeared in the *St. Petersburg (Fla.) Times*, © 1997.

I walked onto the labor and delivery floor just after six A.M. on December 19, 1996. I remember thinking how quiet it was, and how even the sound of my voice at the nurses' desk seemed somehow too loud and conspicuous.

My husband, David, was still at home, taking care of our nineteen-month-old son, Joshua. He would soon be joining me.

A few minutes later, when a nurse breezed in and saw me sitting on the bed, she looked puzzled. "Who's the patient?" she asked.

"Me," I said, bracing for what I knew would come. I caught her eyes covertly sweeping my four-and-a-half-months pregnant belly.

I prayed she would just go look at my chart. I knew if I opened my mouth I would start to cry.

She left the room. When she returned, she obviously had been briefed. Someone had put a sign on the door warning visitors away. Apparently the word had spread. I was there to lose my baby.

I Am a Statistic

It has been more than twenty-five years since the U.S. Supreme Court decided in *Roe v. Wade* that abortion was largely a private matter between doctor and patient. Much of the complexity of this deeply personal issue has been lost over the years in the thunder about morality and reproductive rights. These days most of the hue and cry is focused on second- and third-trimester abortions. . . .

I find it nearly impossible to listen to either side of the abortion argument now that I am a statistic.

Of the approximately 1.4 million abortions performed in this country each year, an estimated 1 percent are on women more than halfway through their pregnancies. I was one of these women.

Perhaps it is true, as some insist, that there are women who simply decide one day, after having gone through most of their pregnancy, that they no longer want the baby. Even a leading abortion-rights advocate admitted in early 1997 that his side had understated the numbers of such cases so as not to lose sympathy for the cause. Still, I find it hard to believe that such casualness is any more common than women who abandon newborns in trash bins or parents who beat their crying children to death.

A Rare Condition

For me, it all began in November 1996, in the sixteenth week of my second pregnancy. I was scheduled to undergo an amniocentesis because of my age. I was thirty-nine.

During a preliminary ultrasound, one of the technicians found a slight blur on the back of the baby's neck. She summoned the doctor and I began to hyperventilate. I choked out the question: "Spina bifida?" The doctor said maybe.

Of course, my first thought was of divine retribution. I was being punished because I had entertained the thought, during bouts of morning sickness and exhaustion, that I didn't really want another child. But any ambivalence vanished in that moment. I wanted this baby more than anything in the world.

From there we embarked on a six-week roller-coaster ride of hope and despair. We saw specialists at a rate of two a week. I stopped working. I didn't sleep. There were five ultrasounds in four weeks. I hyperventilated at all of them.

Our baby boy was diagnosed with a very rare condition called cystic hygroma. A growth on the back of his neck had collected fluid because his lymphatic system had failed to form properly in the second month.

We read every medical journal we could find on this mysterious condition. The pictures were hideous. For the type of cystic hygroma our baby had, the fatality rate was 96 percent.

Holding On

Still, we held on. On a good day, I went to the store and bought wallpaper for the nursery. On a bad day, I threw out an unopened package of maternity panty hose. We named our baby Daniel because I needed to reassure myself he was an infant, not a medical condition. He reminded me by starting to kick.

Cystic hygromas are usually associated with chromosome abnormalities and severe organ defects. As we waited for the amniocentesis results, we decided that if the chromosomes were abnormal, we would end the pregnancy. The test came back normal.

At the third ultrasound, one of the specialists said she thought the hygroma might be shrinking. Sometimes they go away entirely, she told us, but warned that we shouldn't get our hopes up. I wrapped myself in David's arms and wept. I told him I could go on if he could. On Thanksgiving, we toasted our family of four.

But in my twentieth week of pregnancy, the same specialist said no, the hygroma was not shrinking after all. Her face clouded in a way I had come to know all too well. She summoned another doctor and finally told us she was having trouble finding all four chambers of the baby's heart. She sent us to a pediatric cardiologist.

For an hour and a half he scanned my belly. Swallowing the panic was making my chest hurt. I held my husband's hand. I tried to think about the errands I needed to run.

But I knew what he was going to say. The cardiologist told us that one of the chambers was missing and our baby had a large hole in his heart.

Further Complications

Some people might have been able to go on. Our baby was alive and still growing. We will never know what might have been. All we could do was weigh the information we had. The best-case scenario the doctors gave us was that our baby would need at least three immediate surgeries for any hope of survival: two on his heart and one to repair the damage done by the cystic hygroma. That was, if he lived through the birth, or if he even made it to term.

There was another complication. We lived in Florida at the time, and by state law, you can voluntarily terminate a pregnancy only up until the twenty-fourth week.

Cystic hygromas often worsen over time, with serious or fatal complications showing up at the end of the second or even into the third trimester. The only way I could legally wait and still terminate the pregnancy was if my life was in danger. There was nothing wrong with me. We were running out of time.

So we decided it was over. It is something you know not in your mind, but in your heart. Looking back, I realize our doctors had begun gently pointing us in that direction. The cardiologist called us that night to tell us he would have made the same decision. My obstetrician reminded me that I also had Joshua to think of.

I checked into the hospital the following week.

No Absolutes

I used to think I was absolutely sure of where I stood in the abortion debate. Now the only thing I'm sure of is that there are no absolutes.

What I feel most these days is a lingering anger at the intractability on both sides. Why are they each so afraid to admit that the other might have a point? Why is the rhetoric always either inflammatory or coldly medical, as if to use other words would somehow represent lost ground?

Defending Access to Abortion

Those who argue that the current abortion law is riddled with eugenic assumptions undeniably have a point. The law was constructed on the assumption that abortion should be available in circumstances where doctors believe that a woman's capacity for good motherhood is undermined by her health or her circumstances, or that it would be better for society if her child were not born. The current abortion law is not the kind of law that women need. We need access to abortion on request—for whatever reason *we* think is important to defend the access to abortion that current legislation gives us— including access to late abortion for fetal handicap—and to celebrate rather than condemn the use of medical technology that allows women the chance to make a choice.

Ann Bradley, *Living Marxism*, September 1995.

Yes, I am forever thankful for the legal choice to end the life of a baby that I believed had no chance. I believe completely that that right should always be there. More than ever, I am horrified by the idea that some politician with an agenda could take away such an intensely private decision.

Yet, I can no longer accept that it is all as simple as a choice I get to make because it is my body. With choice comes responsibility. This was not some nonviable collection of cells and tissue inside of me. It was a little boy who deserved to be considered.

Because I was twenty-one weeks pregnant, the medical protocol called for labor to be induced so I could deliver the baby stillborn. It was not the partial-birth abortion that so many are focused on these days. It was to be a routine vaginal delivery—four months too soon.

It took over fourteen hours for me to give birth.

The social workers and nurses had tried to prepare us for what was to come. They encouraged us to hold the baby after he was born. They said it was important for the grieving process. Daniel weighed just under a pound. At first I did not think I would be able to look at him. But then I knew I had to. To this day I can close my eyes and still see him. . . .

Supportive Voices

Perhaps there will be those who judge us. Certainly David and I have judged ourselves. Still, I'm not sure anyone can fully understand the path to our decision unless they have walked it. They weren't there, searching each doctor's face for good news and finding none, or in the hospital as I told my tiny baby how sorry I was he would never meet his older brother.

Shortly after we lost our son, I wrote our story for the *St. Petersburg Times*, the newspaper in Florida where my husband and I both worked. The response was astounding—it was overwhelmingly in support of our decision. Several women wrote to tell me that they had made the same choice, but had never been able to talk about it. One woman said that immediately after reading our story she was swept back to the day twenty-five years ago when she knelt in a hospital chapel and prayed to God to end the suffering of her newborn. Another said she had kept the blankets and tiny knitted hat of the child she lost. She had not had the courage to look at those things until now.

But it was the anonymous phone call I received that meant the most to me. It was from a woman who said that she had always believed that terminating a pregnancy was wrong, no matter what. But after reading my story, she told me, she realized it's not that simple.

Almost a year to the day after losing my son, I gave birth to another healthy, happy little boy named Quinn. In my heart he will always be my third child. My second was named Danny.

"We must craft a persuasive moral case against killing the weak and vulnerable."

Congenital Defects Do Not Justify Abortion

Charles W. Colson

Congenital defects do not justify abortion, argues Charles W. Colson in the following viewpoint. Colson, the grandfather of an autistic child, maintains that aborting a fetus because it may be born with severe disabilities is reprehensible. Mentally and physically handicapped people often lead happy lives and challenge others to confront the significance of their own limitations and shortcomings. No one should have the right to decide that such lives are worthless, he concludes. Colson is a contributing editor of *Christianity Today*.

As you read, consider the following questions:

1. According to Colson, what percentage of women abort their pregnancies after discovering that they are carrying a Down syndrome baby?
2. What kinds of arguments are used to encourage women to abort Down syndrome pregnancies, according to the author?
3. According to Tucker Carlson, cited by Colson, what kind of life can the average Down syndrome child expect to lead?

Reprinted, by permission of the author, from Charles W. Colson, "Why Max Deserves a Life," *Christianity Today*, June 16, 1997.

"**S**it in Grandpa's chair." The laughing voice rises from my office chair as Max bounces up and down. Max is my six-year-old grandson, and his visits are a whirl of Mc-Donald's Happy Meals and rambunctious splashes in the pool.

When strangers see Max for the first time, they're immediately drawn to the blond, tousle-haired youngster. But in a few moments, they also notice that Max is different. You see, Max is autistic.

And today kids not very different from Max are being targeted for elimination.

Prenatal testing has become so sophisticated that doctors can now identify many disabilities before birth. But since most have no cure, the only way to "prevent" the disability is to prevent the baby's birth. Thus abortion is bringing back eugenics—the idea of weeding out "defectives" and upgrading our genetic stock.

Consider: In 1990 Joycelyn Elders said that abortion "has had an important, and positive, public-health effect" by reducing "the number of children afflicted with severe defects." Here was a public health official praising "the eugenic utility of abortion," notes Tucker Carlson in the *Weekly Standard*. Abortion is cast not merely as a private choice but also as a way to improve the species.

The Case of Down Syndrome

Take the case of Down syndrome. Studies reveal that when pregnant women learn they are carrying a Down syndrome baby, 90 percent have an abortion. Many say they are acting under pressure from doctors and insurance companies. In a Canadian study, one in three of the mothers said she felt "more or less forced" to abort.

The arguments wielded to "force" women are often crassly economic. Nachum Sicherman of Columbia Business School calls abortion of Down syndrome babies "a great cost saving." Dr. Mark Evans, director of Detroit's Center for Fetal Diagnosis and Therapy, observes that prenatal screening costs $1,000, whereas the first year of a Down syndrome baby's life costs about $100,000. How many couples, facing such staggering costs, are tough enough to withstand the pressure?

And if we don't catch all defective babies before birth,

some doctors have recommended letting them die after birth. A 1975 poll found that 77 percent of American pediatric surgeons favored withholding food and medical treatment from Down syndrome newborns. And some have done just that, as we know from highly publicized cases like the 1982 Baby Doe decision in Indiana.

Special-Needs Children Are in Demand

Ironically, eugenics is making a comeback just as it has become possible for Down syndrome and other special-needs children to lead fairly normal lives. The average Down syndrome child in America today, Carlson writes, is only mildly to moderately retarded. He can expect to attend school, learn to read, hold a job, and to live independently.

In fact, while these children are being targeted for elimination, one adoption agency can't keep up with the demand for them. "It's not at all difficult" to find homes, Janet Marchese of the Down Syndrome Adoption Exchange told Carlson. Her waiting list rarely dips below 100. *World* magazine recently told the touching story of a couple who adopted two Down syndrome children.

What do these couples know that doctors don't? They know children like Max. When Max was diagnosed as autistic, I agonized for my daughter, Emily. But he has turned out to be, quite simply, a great blessing to both of us

"Max is bright, charming, witty, creative," Emily wrote in a letter. It's just that these talents are "channeled in a different way for him." And "different" is sometimes better. "Max seems to appreciate the joy of life more than most of us," Emily wrote. "He brings so much to those around him because of his joyous spirit and exuberance for life. He is a constant reminder of the simple pleasures the rest of us have forgotten."

A Profound Truth

Raising a child with special needs has transformed my little girl into a mature Christian woman. "I imagine that when God created Max, He took him straight from His heart, cupped him in His hands, and set him down on this earth," Emily wrote. But "God knew when He created Max that he would need extra help. So God keeps His hands cupped around Max. . . . How could a child who is held by God be anything but a gift?"

"The Handicapped" Have Names and Faces

My youngest daughter is ten years old. Developmentally, however, she is more like an infant. She does not speak in words, cannot feed or dress herself, wears diapers and cannot walk without assistance. Hearing this litany of what she cannot do, many people would say it would have been better if she had not been born.

A few weeks ago, I attended a national conference on mental handicaps. Most of the participants were special needs professionals; many were parents. At one of the scientific sessions, a physician spoke about the remarkable strides which have been made in pre-natal testing, making it possible to detect a whole host of genetic disorders in the womb. Now, of course, she said ominously, the "decision" can be made by the parents.

Her smug certainty that any "normal" parent would choose to get rid of a baby known to have some disability infuriated me. But what I found really astonishing was the temerity that allowed her to say such things to *us*, people who actually love and cherish the very children she is targeting for destruction. For us, they are not "the handicapped." They have names and faces. They have their winning ways, their sweet charms, their difficult behavior patterns. They are our children and here she was telling us we had missed the boat by having them too soon, before the technology existed which would have allowed us to get rid of them.

Jo McGowan, *Human Life Review*, Spring/Summer 2000.

The experience has taught Emily a profound truth: that "God does not define us by our limitations and shortcomings." If he did, where would any of us be? Some of us are handicapped genetically, others by injury or illness. Some are physically healthy but suffer crippling emotional pain; still others are twisted spiritually by pride or by ambition

Kids like Max force us to confront ourselves. He is a visible reminder that every one of us is broken and fallen, desperately in need of God's redeeming grace.

Humility about our own shortcomings is the spiritual counter to eugenics. Of course we must craft a persuasive moral case against killing the weak and vulnerable. But we must also pray for spiritual wisdom—for a spirit of humility that refuses to play God and arrogate to ourselves the right to judge these lives worthless.

Emily is devoted to helping people understand children like Max. And as for those who believe such children should be eliminated, I say they are going to have to fight my daughter—and fight me.

For Max, Grandpa's chair will always be there.

"One of the most important consequences [of abortion] is the declining violent crime rate."

Abortion Has Led to a Decrease in Crime

Henry Morgentaler

In the following viewpoint, Henry Morgentaler contends that legal abortion has led to a reduction in violent crime. In both Canada and the United States, the number of assaults, rapes, and murders has been decreasing since the early 1990s, Morgentaler explains. Because women have had access to legalized abortion since 1973, fewer unwanted children have been born. Unwanted children are more likely to be neglected and abused and, therefore, to grow into adults who commit acts of violence, he points out. Since less of these children are being born, the crime rate has decreased, he concludes. Morgentaler, a physician, is a prominent Canadian abortion provider.

As you read, consider the following questions:
1. In the author's view, why are abused children more likely to exhibit violent behavior as adults?
2. What do most serial killers have in common, according to Morgentaler?
3. In the author's opinion, what benefits do women enjoy as a result of legalized abortion?

Reprinted, by permission of the author, from Henry Morgentaler, "Abortion and Violence," *The Humanist*, March/April 1999.

At a time when access to safe, medical abortion is being threatened by murderous attacks on doctors providing this service, it would be worthwhile to recapitulate the enormous benefits brought about by legal abortion. I think one of the most important consequences is the declining violent crime rate. This decline has lasted for six years in Canada and the United States.

Fewer Youths Have Inner Rage

Is there a relationship between the statistically proven decline in crime rates and access to abortion? Since 1993, in both the United States and Canada, the crime rate has steadily decreased—in particular for crimes of violence, such as assault, rape, and murder. Some demographers explain this by the fact that there are fewer young men around, and it is mostly young men who commit crimes. No doubt this is true, but what is even more important is that, among these young men likely to commit offenses, there are fewer who carry an inner rage and vengeance in their hearts from having been abused or cruelly treated as children.

Why is that? Because many women who a generation ago were obliged to carry any pregnancy to term now have the opportunity to choose medical abortion when they are not ready to assume the burden and obligation of motherhood. It is well documented that unwanted children are more likely to be abandoned, neglected, and abused. Such children inevitably develop an inner rage that in later years may result in violent behavior against people and society. Crimes of violence are very often perpetrated by persons who unconsciously want revenge for the wrongs they suffered as children. This need to satisfy an inner urge for vengeance results in violence against children, women, members of minority groups, or anyone who becomes a target of hate by the perpetrator.

Children who are given love and affection, good nurturing, and a nice, supportive home atmosphere usually grow up to become caring, emotionally responsible members of the community. They care about others because they have been well cared for. Children who have been deprived of love and good care, who have been neglected or abused, suffer tremendous harm that may cause mental illness, difficulty in living, and an inner rage that eventually erupts in violence when they become adolescents and adults.

Preventive Medicine

Most serial killers were neglected and abused children, deprived of love. Both Hitler and Stalin were cruelly beaten by their fathers and carried so much hate in their hearts that, when they attained power, without remorse they caused millions of people to die. It is accepted wisdom that prevention is better than a cure. To prevent the birth of unwanted children through family planning, birth control, and abortion is preventive medicine, preventive psychiatry, and prevention of violent crime.

Not Such a Puzzle

After *Roe*, women who knew they weren't ready or able to raise children, had a choice. The children they did have were more likely to be wanted.

Today the abortion rates are at their lowest point since *Roe*. That doesn't mean we're due for a crime wave in 2020. It means there are fewer unwanted pregnancies today—due in large part to contraceptives. If there's universal agreement on anything in the world of reproduction, it's that birth control is a better way to prevent "unwantedness" than abortion.

Researchers Steven Levitt and John Donohue set out to answer questions about crime and ended up raising hackles about abortion. Their thesis may or may not hold up to further review. But all in all, it has the whiff of common sense.

As Levitt offers simply enough, "I think children have better outcomes when mothers want them and have the resources and inclination to have them." It's what family planners have said all along. It's not really such a puzzle.

Ellen Goodman, *Liberal Opinion Week*, August 23, 1999.

I predicted a decline in crime and mental illness thirty years ago when I started my campaign to make abortion in Canada legal and safe. It took a long time for this prediction to come true. I expect that things will get better as more and more children are born into families that want and desire them and receive them with joy and anticipation.

It is important that we continue as a society to safeguard the rights and access of women to safe, medical abortion. Not many people realize the enormous benefits to women's health resulting from such good access:

- Disappearance of deaths due to illegal abortions.
- Reduced complication rate attending upon medical abortion, which has become one of the safest surgical procedures.
- Decreased mortality of women giving birth.
- Decreased mortality of babies during childbirth.

Add to this the decrease in crime rates and, most probably, although not statistically proven yet, a significant decrease in mental and emotional illness.

When Canada is rated first in the world by a United Nations agency as to quality of life, part of the rating is due to the increased safety of women due to good access to quality abortion care.

"Since Roe [v. Wade], both abortion and illegitimacy have soared, with doleful effects on crime."

Abortion Has Not Led to a Decrease in Crime

Mona Charen

A 1999 study concluded that legalized abortion has lowered the U.S. crime rate because fewer unwanted children—people who are more likely to become criminals—are being born. This study is flawed, contends syndicated columnist Mona Charen in the following viewpoint. Although it is true that overall crime rates have dropped, a closer look at statistics actually reveals a higher murder rate among people who were born in the first few years after abortion was legalized. It is more likely that the rise and fall of the crack cocaine epidemic—not abortion—is responsible for the apparent decrease in crime since the early 1990s, Charen concludes.

As you read, consider the following questions:
1. According to Steve Sailer, cited by the author, which generation is responsible for the biggest youth crime rampage in U.S. history?
2. By how much did the youth murder rate increase for black males born between 1975 and 1979, according to the author?
3. In what way might abortion actually cause an increase in crime, in Charen's opinion?

Everyone has heard by now of the study purporting to show that legalized abortion has been at least partly responsible for the drop in crime we have been experiencing nationwide. Initial reaction ranged from cautious (from those who believe it) to contemptuous (from those who don't). Could it be, many wondered, that Steve Levitt of the University of Chicago and John Donohue III of Stanford are recommending prenatal capital punishment?

If we can take them at their word, they were simply searching for truth. The question is: Does the study illuminate the drop in crime, or simply play upon unspoken prejudices in the minds of most educated people? Steve Sailer makes an extremely persuasive case in the online magazine Slate (the liveliest site on the Internet) that the study is quite flawed.

Crime Rates

Levitt and Donohue began with a postulate: 1) that legalized abortion results, by definition, in fewer unwanted babies being born, and 2) that since unwanted children are more likely to grow up to be criminals than others—an assumption bolstered by plenty of data—then abortion should lead to lower crime rates.

They tested this hypothesis by examining crime rates in the years after *Roe vs. Wade* became law. Eighteen years after *Roe*, they conclude, crime began to drop. Moreover, in the five states that legalized abortion in 1970, three years before *Roe*, crime rates began to fall three years earlier. Levitt and Donohue further found that those states that had high abortion rates in the mid-1970s experienced greater decreases in crime in the 1990s than states that had low abortion rates in the 1970s.

Not so fast, says Sailer, businessman, gadfly and intellectual jack-of-all-trades. If Levitt and Donohue are correct, the kids who managed to get born despite legalized abortion should have been more law-abiding than previous generations. Instead, they launched the greatest youth crime spree in American history. According to FBI statistics, the murder rate for 1993's crop of 14- to 17-year-olds (who were born in the freely available abortion years of 1975 to 1979) was 3.6 times that of the children born between 1966 and 1970 (pre-*Roe*).

If abortion reduces crime, Sailer continues, then the lower crime rates should have shown up first among the youngest (the wanted babies). But instead, the crime rate drop began among those ages 35 to 49.

The 1980s Crack Epidemic

The 800-pound gorilla that Levitt and Donohue ignore, Sailer insists, is the crack epidemic that transformed urban neighborhoods in the 1980s. Looking at black males born between 1975 and 1979, Sailer notes that their youth murder rate grew 5.1 times. And although black women have abortions at three times the rate of white women, the black juvenile murder rate grew relative to the white rate, from five times worse in 1984 to 11 times worse in 1993.

Abortion and Crime

It's possible that legalized abortion increased crime by contributing to family breakdown. In a 1996 study, economists George Akerlof of the Brookings Institution and his wife, Janet Yellen, until recently the chairman of the Council of Economic Advisers, argued that *Roe v. Wade* and contraception had helped cause the explosion of single-parent families. Men felt less responsible for the children they fathered, because women could avoid or abort pregnancies. "Shotgun marriages" virtually vanished.

The truth is that we don't know the truth. Even if John Donohue and Steven Levitt [the researchers who found a possible link between abortion and lower crime rates] are correct, the abortion debate should remain one of moral values. There are other ways to avoid unwanted children: abstinence, birth control. But it's delusional to pretend that something as common as abortion is without social consequences.

Robert J. Samuelson, *Newsweek*, September 6, 1999.

It was the waxing and waning of the crack epidemic—including better policing, more prisoners, more deaths and more youths in wheelchairs—that accounts for the rise and fall of crime, Sailer believes. A large percentage of the national statistics come from just a few large states, including New York and California, which legalized abortion early but also experienced the worst of the crack epidemic. The good news is that youths born in the early 1980s have shown the biggest decline in murder. Perhaps seeing their older brothers maimed and killed has scared them straight.

Sailer contends that many abortion advocates secretly believe that undesirable people are aborted. He offers a different hypothesis. Suppose that sober, upstanding middle-class blacks are having the abortions, while drug-addicted, disorganized, black mothers are not? Suppose further that legalization of abortion has made underclass women even more careless about birth control than they were pre-*Roe* (Levitt and Donohue's study itself suggests that up to 75 percent of fetuses aborted in the 1970s would never had been conceived without *Roe*). In that case, Sailer contends, the sheer number of unwanted babies conceived might overwhelm the supposed "beneficial" effect of free abortion.

Finally, two capping arguments: Abortion-on-demand spelled the end of the shotgun wedding and, derivatively, of male responsibility. Since *Roe*, both abortion and illegitimacy have soared, with doleful effects on crime. And it is just possible, in a culture that condones the rampant destruction of unborn babies, that youngsters fail to see the moral outrage of shooting born ones.

Periodical Bibliography

The following articles have been selected to supplement the diverse views presented in this chapter. Addresses are provided for periodicals not indexed in the *Readers' Guide to Periodical Literature*, the *Alternative Press Index*, the *Social Sciences Index*, or the *Index to Legal Periodicals and Books*.

Ann Bradley	"Why Shouldn't Women Abort Disabled Fetuses?" *Living Marxism*, September 1995.
Jennifer Braunschweiger	"'My Father Was a Rapist,'" *Glamour*, August 1999.
Christopher Caldwell	"Pro-Lifestyle: Why Abortion Is Here to Stay," *New Republic*, April 5, 1999.
Gregg L. Cunningham	"Wave of the Future?" *National Review*, November 10, 1997.
Rory Evans	"Lifesaving Abortions Denied: My Pregnancy Would Have Killed Me," *Glamour*, February 1999.
Gloria Feldt	"That's One Theory," *Ms.*, December 1999/January 2000.
Sjef Gevers	"Third Trimester Abortion for Fetal Abnormality," *Bioethics*, July 1999. Available from 350 Main St., Malden, MA 02148.
Marguerite Holloway	"The Aborted Crime Wave?" *Scientific American*, December 1999.
Rosalie Maggio	"Partial-Truth Abortion," *Ms.*, June/July 2000.
Denyse O'Leary	"No Room in the Womb?" *Christianity Today*, December 6, 1999.
Stacy Perman	"The Unforseen Effect of Abortion," *Time*, August 23, 1999.
Wendy Shalit	"Whose Choice? Men's Role in Abortion Decisions," *National Review*, May 18, 1998.

CHAPTER 4

Is Abortion Safe?

Chapter Preface

In September 2000, the Food and Drug Administration (FDA) approved the sale of the drug mifepristone, also known as RU-486, for use in nonsurgical abortions occurring within the first seven weeks of pregnancy. The procedure entails a two-drug combination: Mifepristone causes the uterus to shed its lining and dislodge the embryo; then misoprostol, taken two days later, induces contractions that expel the remaining tissue. While abortion rights supporters hailed the FDA's announcement as a breakthrough for American women, opponents condemned it as a move that would endanger human life and health.

Supporters maintain that RU-486 is an effective alternative to surgical abortion, and it provides women a sense of privacy and control during the process of terminating a pregnancy. Although its side effects include nausea, bleeding, and abdominal cramps, several surveys have concluded that more than 95 percent of the women who have had RU-486 abortions would recommend the method to others. Since the procedure requires no anesthesia and carries no risk of uterine perforation or post-surgery infection, many proponents contend that it is generally safer than surgical abortion. "It might be painful, I might bleed," comments one woman who took RU-486, "but it will be more natural; my body will be doing it to itself."

Critics, however, argue that the promoters of the "abortion pill" have downplayed the severity of its side effects. Research scientist Lawrence F. Roberge reports that mifepristone can cause prolonged bleeding and suppress the immune system, increasing the risk for bacterial infections. In addition, misoprostol can induce very painful uterine contractions, and some women are emotionally traumatized when they see the remains of the aborted embryo. "There is nothing easy *or* safe about RU-486," maintains abortion opponent Marian Wallace. "Chemical abortions . . . will *not* advance women's health. They will only advance our national tragedy of abortion."

The viewpoints in the following chapter present further debate about the physical and emotional effects of abortion.

"The physical damage wrought by abortion is well-documented. . . . The emotional harm done to abortive women is also well-known."

Abortion Harms Women

Leslie Carbone

Abortion is harmful to women, argues Leslie Carbone in the following viewpoint. Physical injuries, medical complications, and even deaths have resulted from legal abortions, she points out. Carbone also maintains that many women experience long-term grief and psychological problems after an abortion. In addition, she asserts, the abortion-promoting culture of the United States encourages women to hate their bodies and reject their natural capacity for nurturing. Carbone is a domestic policy analyst at the Family Research Council, an educational organization that promotes traditional Judeo-Christian values.

As you read, consider the following questions:
1. What are some of the physical complications of abortion, according to Carbone?
2. According to the author, how does suicide rate for women who have had abortions compare with the suicide rate for women who have given birth?
3. In Carbone's opinion, how has abortion affected relationships between men and women?

Reprinted, with permission, from Leslie Carbone, "Abortion Lies," 1998, found on the Family Research Council's website at www.frc.org/articles.

A baby is delivered, feet first, up to his neck. A doctor takes a pair of scissors and stabs the back of his tiny head. Next, he suctions the baby's little brains out. The dead infant's body is quickly discarded.

During the struggle to ban partial-birth abortion, those who took the side of life focused chiefly on the inhumanity of such cold-blooded killing of innocent babies. We were right to do so.

The Other Victim

Even so, there is another victim. How can a woman submit to the brutal murder of her own child—while his whole body or just his head is still inside her—and not be scarred by it, if not physically, then certainly emotionally? How can a culture tell women that this act of violence, terminating a normal, natural condition of womanhood, is good for them without inevitably teaching them that their own nature is dangerous to them? How can girls grow into womanhood in such a culture and not be tainted by some degree of doubt and distrust of their own feminine nature, not feel some sense of insecurity, shame, self-disgust?

The physical damage wrought by abortion is well-documented. Twenty-five years of "safe, legal" abortion have left women physically damaged, and sometimes killed, by complications including uterine perforation, cervical laceration, hemorrhaging, anesthesia reactions, and infection (often the result of the use of unclean equipment). A link with breast cancer has been discovered, but other long-term problems are still unknown. Only as the first generation of abortive women ages will we even be able to study the long-term risks of abortion.

The emotional harm done to abortive women is also well-known. Women who have had abortions are three times more likely to commit suicide, within one year of their abortions, than the general population and six times more likely than women who have given birth, according to an article in the *British Medical Journal*. Even as the years put their abortions in the distance, women grieve on each birthday that might have been. They see other women's children of the ages that their own children would be, and they hurt.

A Ghost of a Child

Margaret Liu McConnell, who had an abortion while in college, wrote, "I still carry in my mind a picture of that . . . child who was never born, a picture which changes as the years go by, and I imagine him growing up. . . . [E]very now and then my mind returns to that ghost of a child and to the certainty that for seven weeks I carried the beginnings of a being whose coloring and build and, to a large extent, personality were already determined. Buoyant, green-eyed girl or shy, dark-haired boy, I wonder. Whoever, a child would have been twelve this spring."

Abortion's Link to Breast Cancer

What may link abortion to breast cancer is this: in pregnancy, a woman's body experiences a huge surge of the hormone estrogen—as much as twenty-fold—resulting in dramatic increases in the number of new breast cells. Because of the known link between estrogen and cancer, these rapidly dividing new cells are thought to be particularly susceptible to malignancy. But then something interesting happens. While estrogen begins the process of rapid cell division and tissue growth, a second hormone released during the last trimester shuts it down, allowing the cells to mature and differentiate into specialized cells that can produce milk. This hormone also sorts out and eliminates cells growing out of control, making the woman's breast tissue actually less susceptible to cancer. An abortion, whether performed in a clinic or induced chemically—with RU-486, for example—would interrupt the release of this protective second hormone.

Candace C. Crandall, *Human Life Review*, Fall 1997.

The people who staff so-called family-planning clinics are well aware of the pain, the doubt, and the guilt that abortion causes women, especially when they see children, or even children's things. These clinics serve two constituencies: women seeking surgical abortion and women seeking birth control. Many of the latter constituency already have children, whom they must bring to the clinics when they go for their appointments. Because of this, clinics designate specific days on which to perform abortions and days on which to provide birth control. This allows women seeking surgical abortions to avoid seeing other mothers with their children. Clinic staff will even hide the toys provided for these children to play with while they wait for their mothers, so that immediately pre- and post-abortive women will not be confronted with the sight of these symbols of childhood.

As calculated as it is, this act of shielding aborting women from children's playthings pays unthinking homage to women's nurturing nature. It is bitterly ironic that this is one of the rare remaining signs that this nature is worthy of protection.

Abortion's Message

Abortion's message is that women's unique, natural role is not deserving of honor or protection. This message influences how men view women and how women view themselves. Since the Supreme Court first allowed abortion, our nation has suffered an enormous increase in rape; between 1970 and 1990, the rate of rape increased by 208.6 percent.

Men's sexual exploitation of women is not limited to the extreme case of rape. It is expected of young men, freed by abortion of any social expectation to take responsibility for unplanned pregnancy, to coerce and cajole women into sex. Many women acquiesce under pressure to unwanted sex. Others are rejected or terminate their relationships themselves. Women must be the sexual gatekeepers in their relationships. This means that they are forced to bear the entire weight of moral responsibility in their relationships in a culture that is hostile to virtue. It is an unfair burden, and one that fewer women had to shoulder before *Roe v. Wade*.

Even more insidious is the effect that the abortion culture has had on women's view of themselves. By transforming the most vital, natural role of womanhood into something limiting and dangerous to women, abortion has taught women that our own nature is suspect, even demeaning. Abortion encourages women to view their own bodies as enemy territory. The ravages of this lesson are seen in the increasing rates of self-abuse, such as eating disorders, which flatten the natural shape of a woman's body.

Abortion lies. Its message is that womanhood is devoid of inherent value and that a woman's physical nature is her own enemy. It tells women that our unique role is dangerous to ourselves and valueless to society. It is a lie that far too many women have believed, and they bear the scars, in mind, body, and soul.

| "*Complications from having an abortion in the first three months of pregnancy are considerably less frequent and less serious than those associated with giving birth.*" |

Abortion Is Safe

Susan Dudley

Legal abortion is generally safe for women, explains Susan Dudley in the following viewpoint. Physical complications resulting from legal abortions are relatively rare—particularly with abortions that are performed in the first three months of pregnancy, the author points out. Furthermore, she maintains, most women who have abortions do not experience undue sadness or long-term feelings of guilt. Dudley is an advocate for the National Abortion Federation, a Washington, D.C.–based abortion-rights organization.

As you read, consider the following questions:
1. According to Dudley, what are the physical risks of illegal abortion?
2. What percentage of women experience serious complications from abortions occurring in the first thirteen weeks of pregnancy, according to the author?
3. What emotional reaction do most women report after ending a problem pregnancy, according to Dudley?

From Susan Dudley's "Safety of Abortion," a fact sheet published on the National Abortion Federation's website at www.prochoice.org. Reprinted by permission of the National Abortion Federation, 1755 Massachusetts Ave. NW, Washington, DC 20036.

A bortion is one of the safest types of surgery. Complications from having an abortion in the first three months of pregnancy are considerably less frequent and less serious than those associated with giving birth.

Illegal Abortion Is Unsafe Abortion

Abortion has not always been so safe. Between the late 1800's and 1973, when abortion was illegal in all or most states, many women died or had serious medical problems after attempting to induce their own abortions or going to untrained practitioners who performed abortions with primitive instruments or in unsanitary conditions. Women streamed into emergency rooms with serious complications—perforations of the uterus, retained placentas, severe bleeding, cervical wounds, rampant infections, poisoning, shock, and gangrene.

Around the world, in countries where abortion is illegal, it remains a leading cause of maternal death. In fact, many of the doctors who perform abortions in the United States today are committed to providing this service under medically safe conditions because they witnessed and still remember the tragic cases of women who appeared in hospitals after botched, illegal abortions.

Evaluating the Risks

Since the Supreme Court re-established legal abortion in the U.S. in the 1973 *Roe v. Wade* decision, women have benefitted from significant advances in medical technology and greater access to high quality services. Generally, the earlier the abortion, the less complicated and safer it is. The safest time to have an abortion is between 6 and 10 weeks from the last menstrual period (LMP).

Serious complications arising from abortions before 13 weeks are quite unusual. About 88% of the women who obtain abortions are less than 13 weeks pregnant. Of these women, 97% report no complications; 2.5% have minor complications that can be handled at the physician's office or abortion facility; and less than 0.5% require some additional surgical procedure and/or hospitalization. Complication rates are somewhat higher for abortions performed between

13 and 24 weeks. General anesthesia, which is sometimes used in abortion procedures, carries its own risks.

In addition to the length of the pregnancy, significant factors that can affect the possibility of complications include:

- the skill and training of the provider;
- the kind of anesthesia used;
- the woman's overall health; and
- the abortion method used.

Complications from Legal Abortion

Although rare, possible complications from an abortion procedure include:

- blood clots accumulating in the uterus, requiring another suctioning procedure, which occur in less than 1% of cases;
- infections, most of which are easily identified and treated if the woman carefully observes follow-up instructions, which occur in less than 3% of cases;
- a tear in the cervix, which may be repaired with stitches, which occurs in less than 1% of cases;
- perforation (a puncture or tear) of the wall of the uterus and/or other organs, which may heal itself or may require surgical repair or, rarely, hysterectomy, which occurs in less than 1/2 of 1% of cases;
- missed abortion, which does not end the pregnancy and requires the abortion to be repeated, which occurs in less than 1/2 of 1% of cases;
- incomplete abortion, in which tissue from the pregnancy remains in the uterus, and requires the abortion to be repeated, which occurs in less than 1% of cases;
- excessive bleeding caused by failure of the uterus to contract, which may require a blood transfusion, which occurs in less than 1% of cases.

Between 13 and 16 weeks, the dilation and evacuation (D&E) procedure is significantly safer and more effective than other second trimester abortion methods. After 16 weeks, the different methods carry about the same complication rates.

One death occurs for every 160,000 women who have legal abortions. These rare deaths are usually the result of such things as adverse reactions to anesthesia, heart attacks,

No Link Between Abortion and Cancer

A study published in the *New England Journal of Medicine* on Thursday, January 9, 1997, found no evidence of a link between abortion and breast cancer. The study, by far the largest such study ever published, is being praised by scientists for its freedom from reporter bias, and puts to rest any scientific disputes over the issue. The political dispute, however, may be harder to settle.

Researchers, led by Mads Melbye and Jan Wohlfahrt of the Statens Serum Institut in Copenhagen, reviewed the medical records of over 1.5 million Danish women born between April 1, 1935 and March 31, 1978 (unlike the United States, Denmark maintains detailed medical information for all citizens). Analysis of the medical records revealed that women having abortions within the first 18 weeks of pregnancy showed no increased risk of breast cancer. Overall, the 280,965 Danish women who have had abortions at any stage in pregnancy were no more likely to develop breast cancer than women who had never had abortions.

Adam Guasch-Melendez, Abortion Rights Activist website, 1998.

---

or uncontrollable bleeding. In comparison, a woman's risk of death in carrying a pregnancy to term is ten times greater.

If a woman has any of the following symptoms after having an abortion, she should immediately contact the facility that provided the abortion:

- severe pain;
- chills or fever with an oral temperature of 100.4 or more;
- bleeding that is heavier than the heaviest day of her normal menstrual period or that soaks through more than one sanitary pad per hour;
- foul-smelling discharge or drainage from her vagina; or
- continuing symptoms of pregnancy.

Doctors and clinics that offer abortion services should provide a 24-hour number to call in the event of complications or reactions that the patient is concerned about.

Preventing Complications

There are some things women can do to lower their risks of complications. The most important thing is not to delay the abortion procedure. Generally, the earlier the abortion, the safer it is.

Asking questions is also important. Just as with any medical procedure, the more relaxed a person is and the more she understands what to expect, the better and safer her experience usually will be.

In addition, any woman choosing abortion should:

- find a good clinic or a qualified, licensed practitioner. For referrals, call NAF's toll-free hotline, 1-800-772-9100 or 1-877-4ProChoice;
- inform the practitioner of any health problems, current medications or street drugs being used, allergies to medications or anesthetics, and other health information;
- follow post-operative instructions; and
- return for a follow-up examination.

Anti-abortion activists claim that having an abortion increases the risk of developing breast cancer and endangers future childbearing. They claim that women who have abortions without complications will still have difficulty conceiving or carrying a pregnancy, will develop ectopic (outside of the uterus) pregnancies, will deliver stillborn babies, or will become sterile. However, these claims have been refuted by a significant body of medical research. Furthermore, they are not considered warranted by organizations such as the American Cancer Society, the National Cancer Institute, or National Breast Cancer Coalition.

Women's Feelings After Abortion

Women have abortions for a variety of reasons, but in general they choose abortion because a pregnancy at that time is in some way wrong for them. Such situations often cause a great deal of distress, and although abortion may be the best available option, the circumstances that led to the problem pregnancy may continue to be upsetting.

Some women may find it helpful to talk about their feelings with a family member, friend, or counselor. Feelings of loss or of disappointment, resulting, for example, from a lack of support from the spouse or partner, should not be confused with regret about the abortion. Women who experience guilt or sadness after an abortion usually report that their feelings are manageable. The American Psychological Association concludes that there is no scientifically valid support or evidence for the so-called "post-abortion syndrome" of psychological trauma or deep depression. The most frequent response women report after having ended a problem pregnancy is relief, and the majority are satisfied that they made the right decision for themselves.

"Side effects [of RU-486] will include
infections, bleeding, and delivery of
damaged but viable infants, as well as
long-term health risks."

RU-486 Is Unsafe

Wendy Wright

In September 2000 the Food and Drug Administration approved the drug mifepristone—also known as RU-486—for use with prostaglandin in early nonsurgical abortions. In the following viewpoint, Wendy Wright contends that this "abortion pill" has side effects that are dangerous for women. RU-486 abortions involve more pain, blood loss, trauma, and risky side effects than the drug's promoters have acknowledged, she maintains. Moreover, Wright argues, the Food and Drug Administration's lax standards will result in irresponsible administration of the hazardous drug. Wright is the director of communications for Concerned Women for America, a conservative advocacy organization.

As you read, consider the following questions:
1. According to Wright, why are women who take RU-486 at greater risk for infections?
2. Who will be qualified to administer RU-486, according to the author?
3. Where will RU-486 be manufactured, according to Wright?

Reprinted, with permission, from Wendy Wright, "The Deceit Behind RU-486: Who's Really in Control?" *Family Voice*, November/December 2000.

"Fiona," a 30-year-old divorced mother of two in Great Britain, had previously experienced a surgical abortion. Then she had an RU-486 abortion, and it turned out to be harder than she expected.

"I took the first three tablets," she said. "The process had started and it was inevitable. But you have so long to reflect on it, and I became quite upset.

"The second stage was pretty awful. After taking [the drug to induce contractions], the pain became very strong. It was just like early labor. I remember finally dispelling the fetus. The nurse told me it was 'beautifully formed.'

"[This method] may be physically more natural, but psychologically it hits you much harder. You preside over the killing of a baby, completely unblinkingly."

A Deadly Decision

On September 28, 2000, the Food and Drug Administration (FDA) approved RU-486 (mifepristone) for use in the United States. At a Concerned Women for America press conference held that day, this controversial decision provoked an outcry from doctors, women, legislators and attorneys familiar with the "abortion pill."

The chorus of disapproval—which extends beyond the pro-life community—expressed concern over the drug's dangers, tainted testing, the decision's political timing, and the surprising lack of protections for women.

How could the FDA get it so wrong?

Fox Guarding the Hens

The process of testing and approval in the United States has hardly been impartial. Danco Laboratories has only one product: RU-486. Danco, which was created by the pro-abortion Population Council, holds the patent for RU-486. It raised funds from population-control advocates and relied on testing done by abortion clinics. Pressure from abortion-rights groups and politicians may have led to covering up negative results from U.S. trials.

Dr. Mark Louviere is an emergency room physician in Iowa. He treated a woman in shock from severe blood loss due to an incomplete abortion. Informed that she had been part of the RU-486 clinical trial at Planned Parenthood in Des Moines, Dr. Louviere notified the clinical trial's director and sent the patient's medical record to be included in the study. Yet the trial's report claimed no complications [were] reported among the 238 women who ended unwanted pregnancies without surgery.

"If near death due to loss of half of one's blood volume, surgery, and a transfusion of four units of blood do not qualify as a complication," wrote Dr. Louviere in the *Waterloo* [Iowa] *Courier*, "I don't know what does."

The medical dangers of RU-486 are no secret. In 1995, medical experts, scientists and 24 members of Congress filed a 64-page study with the FDA documenting them. In a petition, they said European data on RU-486 were unreliable, that serious potential complications exist if treatment protocol is not strictly followed, and discussed the lack of long-term studies. The FDA never responded.

Another risk is breast cancer. In 1996, Dr. Joel Brind, a leading researcher on the link between abortion and breast cancer, testified at the FDA's advisory committee hearing on RU-486. He advised the agency then not to approve the drug and repeated his concern at our September press conference. "Of a certainty, thousands upon thousands of women will get breast cancer because they took this drug," Dr. Brind said.

The FDA also failed to acknowledge another common, but rarely mentioned, side effect: infections. Lawrence Roberge, scientist, professor and author of *The Cost of Abortion*, found that RU-486 suppresses a woman's immune system. Combined with the contraction-inducing companion drug (misoprostol), RU-486 renders her body powerless to fight off bacterial infections.

"The problem is further complicated," reported Mr. Roberge, "if the woman using RU-486 has HIV/AIDS or other immunosuppressive diseases, since any infection would almost certainly . . . become a cause for a possible patient death."

A Willing Accomplice

President Clinton has been a key player in RU-486's approval. On his third day in office in 1993, he lifted former

President Bush's ban on the drug and has seemingly accelerated the approval process.

"FDA review time for RU-486 was a mere six months, . . . even faster than the average time for 'fast-tracked' drugs," said Sen. Tim Hutchinson (R–Arkansas) at our press conference. "In this case, the administration rushed a drug through that will take lives instead of save them."

The president and FDA Commissioner Jane Henney insist the decision is one of science and medicine, not politics. However, the FDA ignored scientific information and unanswered questions. Its approval was glaringly void of protections for women.

Who's In Charge Now?

In June 2000, abortion groups leaked to media that FDA approval might come with "limits" or "unprecedented demands on doctors." They didn't need to worry. The FDA's lax requirements allow RU-486 to be "provided by *or under the supervision* of a physician [emphasis added]." This means the physician should know how to determine the pregnancy is no more than seven weeks long and be qualified to diagnose ectopic pregnancies. He or she must be able to provide or refer for surgical abortion when RU-486 fails.

However, the physician can delegate anyone to actually administer the drug. No qualifications were established as to who can work "under the supervision of a physician," leaving the door open for receptionists, janitors, literally anyone to do the deed.

The FDA directs the physician to report babies that survive RU-486 and are not surgically aborted, as well as any hospitalization, transfusion or other complications, to Danco—the very company that has a vested interest in hiding or ignoring them. The FDA's approval relies on two accomplices, the abortionist and the drug marketer, to document problems.

"The FDA's conditions for approval are only recommendations; they are not requirements," said Denise Burke of Americans United for Life, a pro-life legal defense organization. "There are few incentives other than the threat of malpractice lawsuits to prevent physicians from prescribing and using RU-486 in violation of these recommendations."

Further, training of medical personnel about RU–486 falls far short. In 1996, Susan Allen, M.D., who led a company set up by the Population Council, testified before an FDA advisory panel on RU–486. Allen proposed that physicians with no abortion training or experience attend brief seminars to learn to date pregnancies, manage complications, and perform surgical abortions as a back up. Panelist Vivian Lewis, M.D., objected, calling such persons "the worst possible choice." Susan Allen now heads the FDA division that oversees the drug's release.

Risks of RU–486

- Intense pain, nausea, vomiting, diarrhea, headache, back pain, dizziness
- Extreme blood loss. During U.S. trials, four women needed transfusions.
- According to the *New England Journal of Medicine*, 65 women in the study required hospitalization and received surgical intervention and intravenous fluids.
- No long-term studies of the cancerous potential of RU–486 (mifepristone) have been conducted. However, 27 studies worldwide attest to abortion's link to breast cancer.
- There are no studies on the safety of RU–486 for women under age 18 or long-term effects on women's reproductive health.
- Birth defects are possible in the case of an incomplete abortion.

Family Voice, November/December 2000.

The National Abortion Federation (NAF), a trade association of abortionists, has taken the lead in RU–486 training. It has proposed changing the RU–486 protocol practiced in Europe for 12 years. Its suggestion? That women no longer take misoprostol, which follows RU–486 and induces contractions, under a doctor's supervision.

"Having a group of women doing a lot of bleeding and cramping in your office, when they would rather be home, doesn't do much for the [patient] flow in your clinic," said NAF president Dr. Suzanne Poppema.

Made in China

As if side effects, complications and inadequately trained medical personnel weren't enough, women who take RU-486 must also be concerned about where and how the drug is manufactured. The risk that a "healthy" woman would use RU-486 and be injured, or "have a child born with abnormalities," was enough for U.S. drug companies to steer clear of the abortion pill, according to the Reproductive Health Technologies Project.

"As soon as our attorneys learned that it is only 95 percent effective, they began to scream," said one pharmaceutical company executive in *The Political History of RU-486*. "The other 5 percent could involve defective children and that, in terms of liability suits, could blow us out of the water."

So Danco looked to a country known for its contempt for human rights. *The Washington Post* has confirmed Danco has contracted with a company in China to manufacture the pill. Eight senators wrote to the U.S. Secretary of Health and Human Services on September 21, 2000. They asked the FDA to delay a final decision until serious concerns about the manufacturer were answered. Not only do the questions remain unanswered, but the Clinton-Gore administration had allowed the manufacturer to remain secret from the American public.

This development comes in light of recent hearings held in the U.S. House Commerce Committee's Oversight Subcommittee that criticized the FDA for failing to adequately protect the public from dangerously tainted imported drugs. The hearings cited China as a major supplier.

Upon release of the FDA's approval, the response on Capitol Hill was immediate.

"Congress has a duty to ensure that RU-486 kills only one person instead of two," stated Rep. Tom Coburn (R-Oklahoma), who is also a family physician, as he introduced a bill to institute protections for women. "Congress now has the unenviable task of correcting the FDA's mistake."

Going a step further, Dr. Coburn said in this case malpractice suits may succeed where politics may fail. At the press conference, attorney Gerard Mitchell, whose firm has obtained a judgment for more than $7 million for an abortion injury, described medical malpractice claims that may result from RU-486.

"RU-486 is insufficiently studied to be allowed into consumers' hands," Mr. Mitchell warned. "Foreseeable and predictable side effects will include infections, bleeding, and delivery of damaged but viable infants, as well as long-term health risks.

"Counsel for injured women, and for the injured children who survive this terrible drug, will see to it that the truth about RU-486 is told in courtrooms across America. The consequences for those responsible for the distribution of this terrible drug will be severe," he stated.

Physicians, congressmen, scientists, attorneys and women who have been hurt by abortion have all denounced RU-486. Only, it seems, abortion activists celebrated the FDA's approval. But where will they be after RU-486 has done its deadly deed? They claimed the decision was one of "science and medicine." But the evidence indicates it was one of malice toward life. Sooner than later, the truth will be clear.

"Over 620,000 women have safely used mifepristone as an early option for nonsurgical abortion in Europe."

RU-486 Is Safe

National Abortion and Reproductive Rights Action League

The drug mifepristone, commonly known as RU-486, was approved in September 2000 for use in early nonsurgical abortions. In the following viewpoint, the National Abortion and Reproductive Rights League (NARAL) reports that mifepristone is a safe and effective method of abortion. The side effects of RU-486 are not unduly debilitating, and medical complications are rare, NARAL maintains. Many women actually prefer an RU-486 abortion to a surgical abortion because it is a private and noninvasive medical procedure. NARAL, based in Washington, D.C., works to maintain the right of all women to have legal abortions.

As you read, consider the following questions:

1. According to NARAL, how long has mifepristone been in use?
2. For what reason have anti-choice forces attempted to deny access to nonsurgical abortions, in the authors' opinion?
3. According to a study cited by NARAL, what percentage of women who have used RU-486 would recommend it to others?

Excerpted from "Mifepristone and the Impact of Abortion Politics on Scientific Research," a fact sheet published on the website of the National Abortion and Reproductive Rights Action League (NARAL) at www.naral.org/mediaresources/ fact/research.html. Reprinted with permission.

Opposition to the right to choose abortion has impaired medical advances and scientific research in the United States. Use of mifepristone (formerly known as RU 486) in combination with a prostaglandin is an early option for effective, nonsurgical abortion and has been used since 1981. Mifepristone was approved for use in China, France, Great Britain, and Sweden following extensive clinical trials that demonstrated its safety and effectiveness. In addition, in 1999, Austria, Belgium, Denmark, Finland, Germany, Greece, Israel, the Netherlands, and Spain approved mifepristone. Recognizing that mifepristone would expand women's choices and make it more difficult to target abortion clinics for violence and harassment, anti-choice forces have worked to deny women access to nonsurgical methods of abortion.

The Fight for Approval of Mifepristone

During the George Bush Administration, the U.S. Food and Drug Administration (FDA) issued an "import alert" which helped ensure that mifepristone would not be available in the United States for any purpose. A U.S. District Court that examined the "import alert" concluded, "[T]he decision to ban the drug was based not from any bona fide concern for the safety of users of the drug, but on political considerations having no place in FDA decisions on health and safety."

In January 1993, President Bill Clinton signed an Executive Order directing the Department of Health and Human Services to assess initiatives to promote the testing and licensing of mifepristone. From 1994–1995, the Population Council conducted clinical trials on mifepristone in the United States. In 1996, the FDA Advisory Committee for Reproductive Health Drugs recommended approval of mifepristone as a safe and effective nonsurgical method of abortion. In September 1996 and again in February 2000, the FDA issued "approvable letters" for the drug, one of the last procedural steps before final approval. On September 28, 2000, the FDA finally approved mifepristone, for use in combination with misoprostol, as an early option for nonsurgical abortion.

• Over 620,000 women have safely used mifepristone as

an early option for nonsurgical abortion in Europe.

• U.S. clinical trials tested a mifepristone/misoprostol combination that has been used safely and successfully in Europe. The U.S. clinical trials involved 2,100 women across America. The *New England Journal of Medicine* reported in 1998 that a regimen of mifepristone and misoprostol was successful in medically terminating a pregnancy of 49 or fewer days duration in 92 percent of cases, and that the regimen was safe, with side effects consisting of heavy bleeding, cramping, and nausea.

Reprinted by permission of Mike Luckovich and Creators Syndicate.
© Creators Syndicate, Inc.

• In France, where mifepristone is administered up to seven weeks from the start of the last menstrual period, 87 percent of women have complete abortions within three days. Within approximately two weeks, 97 percent of women who receive the drug combination have complete abortions.

The rates were somewhat lower in the U.S. clinical trials, but the study's authors suggest that the 92 percent success rate may be due to lack of provider experience with nonsurgical abortion in the United States as well as to the rigorous design of the study.

• Another recent study based on these clinical trials reports very high patient satisfaction with the regimen: 95.7 percent of women who have used mifepristone would recommend the method to others, and 91.2 percent would choose it again if necessary.

• The process for using mifepristone begins with counseling, a physical examination, and a determination of the length of the pregnancy. At the first visit an initial dose of mifepristone is taken orally. Two days later, a prostaglandin called misoprostol is administered orally or in suppository form. A final visit, approximately twelve days later, verifies that the abortion is complete. If it is not complete, traditional surgical abortion is strongly recommended.

Why Women May Prefer the Abortion Pill

• Women might prefer to use mifepristone over traditional, surgical abortion for a variety of reasons, including that it does not require an invasive procedure or surgery, requires no anesthesia, and does not carry the risk of uterine perforation or injury to the cervix. In addition, many women feel it gives them greater control over the process and increases their privacy. A recent study found that women perceive nonsurgical abortion as a "natural" method—women who choose nonsurgical abortion place importance on the method's resemblance to "a natural miscarriage" and the fact that the abortion can occur at home.

• If the mifepristone/prostaglandin regimen became widely available internationally, it could reduce the estimated 20 million unsafe abortions occurring annually worldwide by giving women an alternative to surgical abortions conducted under dangerously unhygenic conditions. . . .

Anti-Choice Efforts

These significant gains [have been] threatened by the anti-choice majorities in the United States House and Senate. In 1998 and again in 1999, the House adopted an amendment offered by Oklahoma Republican Representative Tom Coburn to bar the FDA from expending any funds to test, develop, or approve drugs that could cause an abortion, such as mifepristone. They cite no precedent for Congress inserting itself into the scientific decision-making process of the FDA to deny Americans access to a safe and effective drug. Although the provision was not enacted, anti-choice forces will likely renew such efforts to reverse the approval of mifepristone.

"After the abortion, a pain begins to emerge from the depths of [a woman's] heart."

Post-Abortion Emotional Problems Harm Women

Paula Vandegaer

Paula Vandegaer, a Catholic nun, is a licensed clinical social worker. She is also executive director of International Life Services and editor of *Living World* magazine. In the following viewpoint, Vandegaer contends that many women experience intense emotional distress and lingering psychological and spiritual problems after an abortion. Such problems, she reports, occur when abortive women attempt to suppress their feelings of maternal grief and shame. According to Vandegaer, post-abortion difficulties can occur many years after an abortion and may include such symptoms as anxiety, substance abuse, promiscuity, eating disorders, emotional withdrawal, and suicidal thoughts.

As you read, consider the following questions:

1. What psychological and physical changes occur a few days after a woman has conceived, according to Vandegaer?
2. According to a study done by Anne Speckhard, cited by the author, what percentage of subjects were surprised about their emotional distress after their abortions?
3. In Vandegaer's opinion, how can abortion hurt those beyond the baby and the mother?

Reprinted, with permission, from Paula Vandegaer, "After the Abortion," online article found at www.hopeafterabortion.com/after.html. © 2000 by the United States Catholic Conference.

Karen is 23. She finished college last year and landed the job of her dreams in graphic arts. The work is creative and challenging. Karen is pretty and has many friends so she is frequently included in the party circuit at work. She should be happy and excited. After all, her life is beginning just as she carefully planned it. But instead, she feels dead and dull inside. She keeps up with her job, but it doesn't bring the joy she thought it would. She feels distant from its satisfactions. She doesn't feel as creative as she once was, and doesn't understand the dull distant sorrowing she feels despite her accomplishments.

Karen had an abortion in college. She thought she had a serious committed relationship with her boyfriend, but when she told him she was pregnant he was definitely less than happy about it. He told her the decision was up to her, but if she wanted an abortion, he would pay for it. She sensed his lack of commitment to her and his baby and decided on abortion. Two of her roommates had abortions and they seemed fine afterwards. What's wrong with her that she feels so depressed about it?

Karen's story is repeated every day on college campuses and in high schools across the country. Since 1973 when the *Roe v. Wade* decision legalized abortion, an estimated twenty-eight million women in the United States have had one or more abortions. These were women who were challenged and stressed by the circumstances surrounding the pregnancy, and the people on whom they normally would rely for support in difficult circumstances were unable, unwilling or unavailable to help with the crisis pregnancy. Boyfriends, even husbands, said they weren't 'ready for fatherhood.' A woman who lacks the willing support and encouragement of the father to help raise the child is more likely to choose abortion.

Society tells young women like Karen that abortion will solve their problem. It says nothing about the problems abortion creates. Supporters of abortion claim it is a simple procedure with no lasting impact. And women who know better don't discuss, certainly not publicly, how abortion changed their lives for the worse. They feel ashamed about the abortion and ashamed about their inability to 'just deal with it' as they think other women do. And so the deception continues.

But if society denies the mother's loss, her body does not. God prepares a woman psychologically and physically for motherhood. When a woman is pregnant she feels different. Within a few days after conception, even before the tiny embryo has nested in her uterine wall, a hormone called 'early pregnancy factor' is found in her bloodstream, alerting the cells of her body to the pregnancy. Her body may now crave different foods, she may need more rest. New cells begin to grow in her breasts, cells which will mature and secrete milk specially formulated for the needs of a newborn. She begins to think 'baby.' She starts noticing babies on the street, in the store, on television. She may dream about her baby at night, and fantasize about her baby during the day. What name? Who will he or she look like?

But if she wants to have an abortion she must try to stop this process. She must deny the maternal feelings entering into her consciousness. She must believe that what is inside of her is not fully a baby. She must stop the process of thinking about her baby as 'her baby.'

But although her mind may say one thing, her emotional life and her body cells say another. If she has the abortion, the very cells of her body remember the pregnancy and know that the process of change that had been going on was stopped in an unnatural manner. Her body and her emotions tell her that she is a mother who has lost a child. And so it is not surprising that after the abortion, a pain begins to emerge from the depths of her heart. She has a loss to mourn, but cannot allow herself to grieve. Grieving would require admitting to herself that a child was killed in the abortion and that she shares responsibility for her child's death. This is a very heavy burden to bear, and so, she resorts to denial in order to cope: denial of the baby's humanity, 'it wasn't a baby so I have nothing to grieve or feel guilty about,' and denial of her emotional pain. 'I should feel okay about this,' she reasons. 'Everyone else does. I must not feel this way or think about the abortion.'

Abortion is an extremely unnatural experience for a woman's body and her maternal instinct. Negative reactions are to be expected and do not depend on a person's religious beliefs or general mental health. It is true that women and men with prior psychological problems or with strong religious beliefs are more vulnerable to post-abortion problems, but there are repercussions for all women involved in an abortion. In a study done by Anne Speckhard, Ph.D, 85% of the women reported that they were surprised at the intensity of their emotional reaction to the abortion. These reactions included discomfort with children, feelings of low self-worth, guilt, feelings of anger, depression, grief, increased alcohol use, crying, inability to communicate and feeling suicidal. Yet 72% of the subjects reported no identifiable religious belief at the time of the abortion.

Post-abortion reactions are specific and identifiable. They originate mainly from the problem of denial and suppression of feelings. When we suppress one of our emotions it affects all of them. This is the basis of post-abortion trauma: the denial of the baby and the denial of our feelings. This causes symptoms of reexperience, avoidance and impacted grieving.

The abortion trauma can be reexperienced in a number of ways. Some women experience recollections and flashbacks of the abortion and dreams of the unborn child. Some experience intense psychological distress from people or things that remind them of the abortion, such as seeing pregnant women or passing an abortion clinic. Intense grieving and depression may occur on the anniversary dates of the abortion or the child's projected due date.

Many examples can be given of reexperiencing. A number of women I have worked with have difficulty having a cervical exam or going into a hospital. These events cause such anxiety that they are no longer able to tolerate them. Many women I know have nightmares about their abortion or the baby. One large Finnish study examining all suicides among women in an eight-year period found that women who had an abortion committed suicide at three times the rate of the general population and almost six times the rate of women who had given birth.

The pro-life pregnancy service centers in the U.S. report that many women come into the centers pregnant again on the anniversary date of the abortion or on the date of the birth of the aborted baby. This may be an attempt to deal with the sadness of these days. A survey of 83 post-abortive women done by Kathleen Franco, M.D. of the Medical College of Ohio, illustrates how widespread is the problem of anniversary reactions. Thirty of the respondents had experienced physical or emotional reactions on the anniversary of the abortion or the due date. These included problems such as suicidal thoughts, headaches, cardiac symptoms, anxiety, alcohol and drug abuse, or more verbal abuse toward their children.

Women also experience avoidance symptoms. These include avoidance of anything associated with the abortion trauma or numbing of the responsiveness that was present before the abortion. These include efforts to avoid or deny thoughts or feelings associated with the abortion; efforts to avoid activities, situations, or information that might cause a remembrance of the abortion; inability to recall the abortion experience or an important aspect of the abortion. Other significant symptoms include very diminished interest in significant activities, feeling of detachment or estrangement from others, withdrawal in relationships or reduced communication. Some women have restricted range of affect [emotion], such as an inability to have loving or tender feelings.

Karen, whom we met in the beginning of this viewpoint, is an example of problems created by avoidance. Although she has a good job and happy lifestyle, because she won't allow her feelings of grief and guilt into consciousness, she cannot experience her full range of emotions. She needs to be on guard not to think about her abortion. As commonly happens, shortly after the abortion the relationship with the boyfriend ended. She could no longer relate to him. Women who have undergone abortion may be grouped as follows: 1) those who are suffering post abortion reactions on an acute or chronic basis; and 2) those who have no identifiable problems now but are at risk at a future 'stress time' (such as a pregnancy, crisis in life, death of a loved one). Reactions may be severe or mild and they can vary over a person's lifetime.

Sadly many women do not seek help for abortion-related problems until about five to twelve years after the abortion. In the intervening time they may suffer profoundly as some of these symptoms may periodically recur. Various methods may be tried to manage the resulting pain: alcohol, prescription drugs and illegal drugs, promiscuity, hyper-activity (workaholism), punishing oneself by being in an abusive relationship or developing eating disorders, for example. Others may attempt to replace the lost baby by becoming pregnant again, and others reenact both the pregnancy and abortion, hoping to make the experience routine and non-traumatic (or to punish themselves). Unfortunately, each of these strategies produces additional pain and problems.

Unresolved Pain

When a group of young professional women gathered to discuss a recent work on women's sexuality, each confessed her reasons for not having begun to read the agreed-upon work. Three of the four attributed their struggle to a particularly painful experience: They had had abortions.

All three women were Catholic by upbringing, if not according to their current spiritual practice, and all were college-age at the time of their abortions. While they generally felt they had made the best decision they could at the time, the three expressed deep, unresolved pain over their abortions and said they struggled to find "forgiveness" for those decisions. Pro-choice rhetoric aside, they appear to have suffered in abortion a deep wound to their womanhood, a wound that also struck at the heart of their spiritual life.

James Bretzke and Monika Rodman, *America*, November 6, 1999.

Sometimes the reaction to abortion is very delayed. As we mature and have an opportunity to reflect on our life, we may regret our past decisions. Counselors sometimes encounter elderly women overcome with grief from the loss of a child to abortion that occurred many decades earlier, a grief that has been buried, more or less successfully, until then. A friend recently told me of a seventy-five year-old woman she knew who sobbed uncontrollably over an abortion that occurred more than fifty years ago. She was never able to have another child and was facing the prospect of living her declining years alone.

Slightly over one-fourth of women (aged 15 and up) in the United States have undergone an abortion. Women, and all those involved in the decision to abort, must believe, or try to believe, that there was no human life present in the womb. To admit this is to admit complicity in the killing of an innocent human being. Condemning abortion would mean condemning themselves or the wife, daughter, sister or friend whom they love. And so society refuses to recognize the incontrovertible facts about human life before birth.

Many people close to a women in a crisis pregnancy don't feel comfortable with the decision to abort, but they don't know what to say. They want to be supportive and non-judgmental, so they say something like, 'You're really in a bad situation and I'll support whatever you decide.' The helpful response, the right response should be, 'Don't have an abortion. I will not abandon you. Together we will find a way for you to have your baby.'

A true story will illustrate how abortion harms others beyond the baby and mother. Joanne and Rob (not their real names) were married and had children. Rob lost his job and they were fast running out of savings when she got pregnant. Joanne felt she should get an abortion. Rob repeatedly begged her not to. Joanne was very ambivalent and decided to seek advice from her mother, whom she felt was a good Catholic and someone she admired.

Joanne's mother listened thoughtfully and in a sympathetic voice said, 'I understand what you are feeling and why you want an abortion. I thought of abortion too in some of my pregnancies, and I can see why you feel it makes sense in this situation. I will support whatever you decide.'

Joanne felt her mother gave her permission for the abortion and so she went through with it. Shortly afterward, Rob got a new job, their financial situation improved, and Joanne went into a severe reaction of grief, anxiety, and guilt that required active psychiatric care. She was very angry, not at her husband who opposed the abortion—but at her mother, whom she expected to stop her. The abortion affected the entire family—the marriage relationship, the other children who knew that a brother or sister was aborted, her relationship with her mother and with other relatives who knew or guessed. Rob had felt helpless, unable to protect his child's life and felt that Joanne had lost confidence in his ability to provide for the family. The abortion taught all of them that this family was not as safe and close as they had thought. They would allow a family member to be sacrificed before they would help one another out with a loan or other assistance. The abortion disrupted the security of the family more permanently than the financial problems ever would.

The Catholic Church has long recognized abortion's impact on women and their families. While law and society often pit the interests of a mother against those of her unborn child, the Church recognizes that their best interests are joined. What is best for the child is also best for the mother.

Project Rachel began over fifteen years ago as an outreach of the Catholic Church to women, men and families who have been affected by abortion. The Church is a place of healing. It speaks the truth about abortion to men and women contemplating this action. 'Don't do it! It is wrong and it will hurt you and the baby,' but it also speaks the full truth: 'If you have had an abortion, God's mercy is great enough to forgive that, too.' Jesus offers forgiveness and healing. He offers the hope and promise of resurrection and reunion with the child who is waiting for his parents in heaven.

People who call Project Rachel are offered referrals to professional counselors or to priests specially trained for spiritual guidance and the Sacrament of Reconciliation. But basically everyone in the Church is a part of Project Rachel. Everyone is a part of the healing ministry of Christ. You may know someone whom you think has had an abortion. You never accuse or confront. A simple word that will touch their hearts and release them from fear and isolation can begin the healing process.

You might say something like, 'You know, I just read this article on post-abortion trauma. It said that women and men who have experienced abortion can suffer for years with remorse, depression, anxiety, nightmares and worry about their decision. Many times they think there is something wrong with them, but in reality they are suffering grief from the loss of their child.' You can go on to explain that the Church has a Project Rachel ministry as a way of healing. Simply giving people information like this can help. Pray that they will eventually talk to someone. In a 'special message to women who have had an abortion' in the Gospel of

Life, Pope John Paul II explains how their lives can be transformed by the Church's healing ministry:

> You will come to understand that nothing is definitively lost and you will also be able to ask forgiveness from your child, who is now living in the Lord. With the friendly and expert help and advice of other people, and as a result of your own painful experience, you can be among the most eloquent defenders of everyone's right to life. Through your commitment to life, whether by accepting the birth of other children or by welcoming and caring for those most in need of someone to be close to them, you will become promoters of a new way of looking at human life.

"Although psychological disturbances do occur after abortion, they are uncommon and generally mild and short-lived."

Post-Abortion Emotional Problems Are Rare

Joyce Arthur

In the following viewpoint, Joyce Arthur maintains that women who have abortions rarely experience serious emotional difficulties or depression afterward. She contends that biased and misleading research has led anti-abortion advocates to claim that a disorder—"post-abortion syndrome"—results in long-term and devastating psychological disturbances among women who have had abortions. More recent and solid evidence, however, reveals that most women who undergo abortion feel relieved and happy about their decision. Arthur is a spokesperson for the Pro-Choice Action Network in Vancouver, Canada; she also edits the Canadian newsletter *Pro-Choice Press*.

As you read, consider the following questions:
1. What kinds of flaws are seen in research studies that favor anti-abortion beliefs, according to Arthur?
2. According to studies cited by the author, what percentage of women report feeling relieved immediately after an abortion?
3. Which women are at greater risk for post-abortion psychological problems, according to Arthur?

Reprinted, by permission of the author, from Joyce Arthur, "Psychological Aftereffects of Abortion: The Rest of the Story," *The Humanist*, March 13, 1997.

O ver the last decade, a consensus has been reached in the medical and scientific communities that most women who have an abortion experience little or no psychological harm. Yet a woman's ability to cope psychologically after an abortion continues to be the subject of heated debates. Vocal anti-abortion advocates claim that most women who have abortions will suffer to some degree from a variant of post-traumatic stress disorder called post-abortion syndrome, characterized by severe and long lasting guilt, depression, rage, and social and sexual dysfunction. Why is there such a major discrepancy between the scientific consensus and anti-abortion beliefs?

Contradictory Studies

Conflicting studies done over the last thirty years have contributed to this atmosphere of confusion and misinformation. A 1989 review article that evaluated the methodology of seventy-six studies on the psychological aftereffects of abortion noted that both opponents and advocates of abortion could easily prove their case by picking and choosing from a wide range of contradictory evidence. For example, many studies—especially those done between 1950 and 1975—purport to have found significant negative psychological responses to abortion. Such studies, though, often suffer from serious methodological flaws. Some were done when abortion was still illegal or highly restricted, thereby biasing the conclusions in favor of considerable (and understandable) psychological distress. In some cases, research was based on women who were forced to prove a psychiatric disorder in order to obtain the abortion. Further, a large number of studies, both early and recent, consist simply of anecdotal reports of a few women who sought psychiatric help after their abortion. In short, many studies which favor anti-abortion beliefs are flawed because of very small samples, unrepresentative samples, poor data analysis, lack of control groups, and unreliable or invalid research questions.

Researcher bias on the part of scientists and physicians has also been a serious problem. In earlier times, society's views on how women "should" feel after an abortion were heavily skewed toward the traditional model of women as nurturing mothers. In one study done in 1973, postdoctoral psychology students taking psychoanalytic training predicted psychological effects far more severe than those predicted by women themselves before undergoing an abortion. This might be because traditional Freudian theory teaches that a desire to avoid childbearing represents a woman' s denial of her basic feminine nature.

Some psychiatric studies, along with much of today's anti-abortion literature, tend to cast women who have abortions into one of two roles: victim or deviant (although these terms are not necessarily used). Victims are coerced into abortion by others around them, in spite of their confusion and ambivalence, and against their basic maternal instincts. Deviants have little difficulty with the abortion decision, which is made casually for convenience sake. Such women have no maternal instinct and are often characterized in a derogatory or pitying fashion as selfish, callous, unfeminine, emotionally stunted, and neurotic.

Biased Psychology

Books written by anti-abortion advocates that deal with post-abortion effects are, by and large, heavily infected with bias. Not only is contrary evidence unrefuted, it is rarely even mentioned. Incorrect and out of date "facts" abound. The authors' pop psychology often seems to be based on little more than their own wishful projections about the nature of women and how they should feel. Here are two typical examples from essays in the 1977 anti-abortion book *The Psychological Aspects of Abortion*:

> It is interesting that women who need self punishment do not abort themselves more often. . . . Abortion is done "to" the woman, with her as only a passive participant. This is further indication of masochism.
>
> Howard W. Fisher, "Abortion: Pain or Pleasure"

> . . . Sooner or later [after the abortion], the truth will make itself known and felt, and the bitter realization that she was not even unselfish enough to share her life with another human being will take its toll. If she had ever entertained a doubt as to whether her parents and others really considered her unlovable and worthless, she will now be certain that she was indeed never any good in their eyes or her own. A deep

depression will be inevitable and her preoccupation with thoughts of suicide that much greater.

Conrad W. Baars, "Psychic Causes and Consequences of the Abortion Mentality"

Post-Abortion Problems Are Uncommon

With the advent of safe, legal, routinely performed abortions, a wealth of good evidence has come to light that is quite contrary to common anti-abortion assertions. The typical abortion patient is a normal, mentally stable woman who makes a strongly resolved decision for abortion within a few days after discovery of the pregnancy and comes through the procedure virtually unscathed. Several scientific review articles—published from 1990 to 1992 in highly respected journals such as *Science* and *American Journal of Psychiatry*—support this conclusion. The reviews evaluated hundreds of studies done over the last thirty years, noting the unusually high number of seriously flawed studies and pointing out common methodological problems. Based upon the more reliable studies, all the reviews concluded that, although psychological disturbances do occur after abortion, they are uncommon and generally mild and short-lived. In many cases, these disturbances are simply a continuation of negative feelings caused by the pregnancy itself. Serious or persistent problems are rare and are frequently related to the circumstances surrounding the abortion rather than the abortion itself.

Further, many women who were denied an abortion showed ongoing, long-term resentment, and their resulting children were more likely to have increased emotional, psychological, and social problems in comparison with control groups of children. These differences between children widened throughout adolescence and early adulthood. Finally, many studies show that giving birth is much more likely than abortion to be associated with severe emotional aftereffects, such as post-partum depression.

The review articles largely concluded that the most frequently reported emotions felt by women immediately following an abortion (experienced by about 75 percent of women) are relief or happiness. Feelings of regret, anxiety, guilt, depression, and other negative emotions are reported by about 5 percent to 30 percent of women. These feelings are usually mild and fade rapidly, within a few weeks. Months or years after an abortion, the majority of women do not regret their decision. In fact, for many women, abortion appears to improve their self-esteem, provide inner strength, and motivate them to refocus their lives in a meaningful way.

Abortion Does Not Cause Emotional Problems

Does abortion ruin a woman's life? Does it have any long-term effects at all? In the vast majority of cases of legal, early abortion, the answer is no, according to psychologist Dr Nancy Felipe Russo of Arizona State University—a conclusion that has caused controversy in the US. Dr Russo participated in a large-scale American review of independent studies of women's responses to abortion by a team of psychologists. The team found that studies claiming women suffer from depression and mental health problems after abortion do not take into account the fact that they may have suffered from diverse other problems beforehand.

"We looked at factors such as education, income, how many children women already had and their levels of self-esteem before the operation, and found that the abortion itself had no independent effect," explains Dr Russo. "If you really care about women's mental health, you won't just talk about abortion, you will look at the complexities of some women's lives—lack of education, no money, a violent partner, sexual abuse, the effects of not having an abortion. There is no relationship of depression to abortion."

Hester Lacey, *Independent on Sunday*, August 3, 1997.

Studies on abortion are done primarily through self-report measures, however, and it is possible that some women may be reluctant to admit negative feelings after their abortion. To help quantify this, consider these figures: every year since 1977, 1.3 million to 1.6 million abortions are performed in the United States; about 21 percent of all American women between the ages of fifteen and forty four have had an abortion. These are very large numbers indeed. The American Psychological Association has pointed out that, even if only 10 percent of the millions of women who have had abortions experienced problems, there would be a significant mental health epidemic, clearly evident by large numbers of dysfunctional women requesting help. There is no evidence of any such epidemic, thereby supporting the general reliability of self-report measures.

Those Who Need Extra Help

Some women who are disturbed or unhappy with their abortion decision belong to support groups like Women Exploited by Abortion and Victims of Choice. Several antiabortion studies and books purporting to demonstrate the overall harmfulness of abortion limit their samples to the membership of such groups. Not only does this introduce an immediate and fatal flaw to their argument, it shows deliberate obfuscation on the part of the authors. This does not mean, however, that post-abortion support groups are valueless to women. The very existence of such groups points to the strong need for health professionals to identify and provide extra help to women who are most at risk for developing psychological problems related to abortion. Many studies have shown that women at greater risk tend to include:

- emotionally immature teenagers
- women with previous psychiatric problems
- women aborting a wanted pregnancy for medical or genetic reasons
- women who encounter opposition from their partner or parents for their abortion decision
- women who have strong philosophical or religious objection to abortion
- women who are highly ambivalent or confused about their abortion decision and had great difficulty making it
- women who are coerced by others into having an abortion
- women undergoing second trimester abortions

In spite of psychological problems suffered by a few women after abortion, the existence of post-abortion syndrome is doubted by most experts. There is little need to posit a unique disorder in this case, since abortion is not significantly different from any other stressful life experience that might cause trauma in certain people. Former Surgeon General C. Everett Koop, himself anti-abortion, noted this in 1988. Unfortunately, facts, evidence, and common sense rarely get in the way of anti-abortion advocates who are determined to prove that women suffer terribly from post-abortion syndrome. Certainly, if this syndrome were real it would be a lethal weapon in the fight to reverse *Roe v. Wade*. This was, in fact, the motivation behind a 1989 surgeon general's report on the health effects of abortion on women, which was called for by former President Ronald Reagan on behalf of anti-abortion leaders. Although the report was duly prepared, the surgeon general chose not to release it, apparently because it did not support the anti-abortion position. Meanwhile, anti-abortion literature continues to churn out the myth that women are severely harmed by abortion.

Because abortion is such a volatile issue, it is probably unrealistic to expect this aspect of the controversy to die down soon, if at all. However, by recognizing that a small subset of women may require increased counseling and support during their abortion decision and afterward, the women's community and health professionals can do much to minimize the damage wrought by the anti-abortion movement's dangerous and irresponsible campaign of misinformation.

Periodical Bibliography

The following articles have been selected to supplement the diverse views presented in this chapter. Addresses are provided for periodicals not indexed in the *Readers' Guide to Periodical Literature*, the *Alternative Press Index*, the *Social Sciences Index*, or the *Index to Legal Periodicals and Books*.

James Bretzke and Monika Rodman	"After the Choice," *America*, November 6, 1999.
Joel Brind	"Abortion, Breast Cancer, and Ideology," *First Things*, May 1997. Available from 156 Fifth Ave., Suite 400, New York, NY 10010.
Candace C. Crandall	"None of Our Business?" *Human Life Review*, Fall 1997. Available from 215 Lexington Ave., 4th Floor, New York, NY 10016.
The Economist	"Abortion, Breast Cancer, and the Misuse of Epidemiology," March 2, 1996.
Nancy Gibbs	"The Pill Arrives," *Time*, October 9, 2000.
Cynthia Gorney	"Abortion Changes, But How Much?" *The New York Times*, September 29, 2000.
Hester Lacey	"Does Abortion Really Ruin Your Life?" *Independent on Sunday*, August 3, 1997.
Katha Pollitt	"A Woman's Body as Political Territory," *Free Inquiry*, Fall 2000.
Anna Quindlen	"RU-486 and the Right to Choose," *Newsweek*, October 9, 2000.
Hanna Rosin	"Pain, Penance, and RU-486," *Washington Post*, October 14, 2000. Available from 1150 15th St. NW, Washington, DC 20071.
Irving M. Spitz et al.	"Early Pregnancy Termination with Mifepristone and Misoprostol in the United States," *New England Journal of Medicine*, April 30, 1998. Available from 10 Shattuck St., Boston, MA 02115-6094.
Susan F. Wills	"Clinical Psychosis," *National Review*, November 23, 1998.

For Further Discussion

Chapter 1

1. The Catholic Bishops of the United States maintain that abortion is immoral because human life begins at conception. Moreover, they believe that Christians are called to defend the sanctity of unborn human life. John M. Swomley argues that the Bible contains no references to the immorality of abortion and that the bishops are imposing their own theological views on the Scriptures. Whose argument do you agree with, and why?

2. Carolyn C. Gargaro contends that abortion is a form of killing because it results in the death of an individual with a complete and unique genetic code. Brian Elroy McKinley, on the other hand, maintains that abortion is not murder because an unborn embryo or fetus cannot live outside of the uterus and is not yet a person. At what point do you believe human life should be granted "personhood?" Why? Use evidence from the viewpoints to support your answer.

3. Gregg Cunningham and Joyce Arthur strongly disagree about defining abortion as a form of genocide. What evidence do Cunningham and Arthur use to support their arguments? In your opinion, whose argument is more credible? Explain.

Chapter 2

1. Michael W. McConnell and Don Sloan strongly disagree about the need for restrictions on abortion rights. In each author's viewpoint, try to find two arguments that you agree with. Why do you agree with them?

2. Glenn Woiceshyn maintains that late-term abortion is an emergency procedure employed when a fetus is severely deformed or when a pregnancy threatens the life of the mother. John Leo contends that late-term abortion is a form of infanticide that is never needed to save the life of the mother. Based on these viewpoints, would you support or oppose legislation that would ban late-term abortions? Why?

3. Charles T. Canady and Eileen Roberts assert that parents have the right to be informed about their daughter's abortion. Jonathan D. Klein maintains that teens should be encouraged to seek their parents' counsel if they become pregnant, but they should also have access to confidential medical care if they are unable to share such information with their parents. Whose argument is more convincing? Why?

Chapter 3

1. Naomi Wolf acknowledges the undesirability of abortion, but maintains that it must remain a legal option for a woman facing an unwanted pregnancy. Clarke D. Forsythe contends that the myth of abortion as a "necessary evil" has distorted public opinion and debate on the issue. Does Forsythe's viewpoint effectively refute Wolf's argument? Why or why not? Use evidence from the text to support your answer.

2. After reading the viewpoints by Margaret Sykes and William Norman Grigg, are you more or less inclined to support a woman's decision to terminate her pregnancy because she has been raped? Explain.

3. Jenny Deam and Charles W. Colson both tell stories from their personal lives to support their respective arguments for and against choosing abortion because of a fetus's congenital defects. In your opinion, who uses their personal experience to better effect?

4. Henry Morgentaler argues that one of the benefits of legalized abortion is that is has led to a decrease in crime rates. In your opinion, is this a satisfactory justification for abortion? Why or why not?

Chapter 4

1. Wendy Wright and the National Abortion and Reproductive Rights Action League (NARAL) agree that RU-486 abortions have painful side effects and require several trips to a doctor's office. Yet Wright argues that the drug is harmful, while NARAL maintains that it is safe. Whose argument do you think is more convincing, and why? Support your answer with evidence from the viewpoints.

2. Paula Vandegaer contends that many women experience long-term emotional problems after an abortion. Joyce Arthur asserts that such emotional difficulties are uncommon and that most women are relieved after an abortion. Vandegaer is a Catholic nun and a director of a pro-life organization, while Arthur is a writer and advocate for pro-choice organizations. Does knowing their backgrounds influence your assessment of their arguments? Explain.

Organizations to Contact

The editors have compiled the following list of organizations concerned with the issues debated in this book. The descriptions are derived from materials provided by the organizations. All have publications or information available for interested readers. The list was compiled on the date of publication of the present volume; the information provided here may change. Be aware that many organizations take several weeks or longer to respond to inquiries, so allow as much time as possible.

ACLU Reproductive Freedom Project
125 Broad St., New York, NY 10004-2400
(212) 549-2500
e-mail: aclu@aclu.org
website: www.aclu.org/issues/reproduct/hmrr.html

A branch of the American Civil Liberties Union, the project coordinates efforts in litigation, advocacy, and public education to guarantee the constitutional right to reproductive choice. Its mission is to ensure that reproductive decisions will be informed, meaningful, and free of hindrance or coercion from the government. The project disseminates fact sheets, pamphlets, and editorial articles. It also publishes the quarterly newsletter *Reproductive Rights Update*.

Alan Guttmacher Institute
120 Wall St., 21st Floor, New York, NY 10005
(212) 248-1111 • fax: (212) 248-1951
e-mail: info@agi-usa.org • website: www.agi-usa.org/index.html

The institute is a reproduction research group that advocates the right to safe and legal abortion. It provides extensive statistical information on abortion and voluntary population control. Publications include the bimonthly journal *Family Planning Perspectives*, which focuses on reproductive health issues; *Preventing Pregnancy, Protecting Health: A New Look at Birth Control in the U.S.*; and the book *Sex and America's Teenagers*.

American Life League (ALL)
PO Box 1350, Stafford, VA 22555
(540) 659-4171 • fax: (540) 659-2856
e-mail: whylife@all.org • website: www.all.org

ALL promotes family values and opposes abortion. The organization monitors congressional activities dealing with pro-life issues and provides information on the physical and psychological risks of abortion. It produces educational materials, books, flyers, and programs for pro-family organizations that oppose abortion. Publications include the biweekly newsletter *Communique*, the bimonthly magazine *Celebrate Life*, and the weekly newsletter *Lifefax*.

Americans United for Life (AUL)

310 S. Peoria St., Suite 300, Chicago, IL 60604-3816
(312) 492-7234 • fax: (312) 492-7235
e-mail: infor.aul@juno.com • website: www.unitedforlife.org

AUL promotes legislation to make abortion illegal. The organization operates a library and a legal-resource center. It publishes the quarterly newsletter *Lex Vitae*, the monthly newsletter *AUL Insights* and *AUL Forum*, and numerous booklets, including *The Beginning of Human Life* and *Fetal Pain and Abortion: The Medical Evidence*.

Catholics for a Free Choice (CFFC)

1436 U St. NW, Suite 301, Washington, DC 20009
(202) 986-6093 • fax: (202) 332-7995
website: www.cath4choice.org

CFFC supports the right to legal abortion and promotes family planning to reduce the incidence of abortion and to increase women's choice in childbearing and child rearing. It publishes the bimonthly newsletter *Conscience*, the booklet *The History of Abortion in the Catholic Church*, and the brochure *You Are Not Alone*.

Center for Bio-Ethical Reform (CBR)

PO Box 8056, Mission Hills, CA 91346
(818) 360-2477 • fax: (818) 360-2477
e-mail: cbr@cbrinfo.org • website: www.cbrinfo.org

CBR opposes legal abortion, focusing its arguments on abortion's moral aspects. Its members frequently address conservative and Christian groups throughout the United States. The center also offers training seminars on fundraising to pro-life volunteers. CBR publishes the monthly newsletter *In-Perspective* and a student training manual for setting up pro-life groups on campuses titled *How to Abortion-Proof Your Campus*. Its audiotapes include "Is the Bible Silent on Abortion?" and "No More Excuses."

Childbirth by Choice Trust

344 Bloor St. West, Suite 306, Toronto, ON M5S 3A7 Canada
(416) 961-1507 • fax: (416) 961-5771
e-mail: info@cbctrust.com
website: www.cbctrust.com/homepage.html

Childbirth by Choice Trust's goal is to educate the public about abortion and reproductive choice. It produces educational materials that aim to provide factual, rational, and straightforward information about fertility-control issues. The organization's publications include the booklet *Abortion in Law, History, and Religion* and the pamphlets *Unsure About Your Pregnancy? A Guide to Making the Right Decision* and *Information for Teens About Abortion*.

Feminists for Life of America
733 15th St. NW, Suite 1100, Washington, DC 20005
(202) 737-3352
e-mail: fems4life@aol.com • website: www.feministsforlife.org

This organization comprises feminists united to secure the right to life, from conception to natural death, for all human beings. It believes that legal abortion exploits women. The group supports a Human Life Amendment, which would protect unborn life. Publications include the quarterly *Sisterlife*, the book *Prolife Feminism: Different Voices*, the booklet *Early Feminist Case Against Abortion*, and the pamphlet *Abortion Does Not Liberate Women*.

Feminist Majority Foundation (FMF)
1600 Wilson Blvd., Suite 801, Arlington, VA 22209
(703) 522-2214 • fax: (703) 522-2219
e-mail: femmaj@feminist.org • website: www.feminist.org

FMF advocates political, economic, and social equality for women. The foundation also strives to protect the abortion right for women. It hosts the National Clinic Defense Project and the Campaign for RU-486 and Contraceptive Research. FMF reports on feminist issues, including abortion, in its quarterly *Feminist Majority Report*.

Human Life Foundation (HLF)
215 Lexington Ave., New York, NY 10016
(212) 685-5210 • fax: (212) 725-9793
website: www.humanlifereview.com

The foundation serves as a charitable and educational support group for individuals opposed to abortion, euthanasia, and infanticide. HLF offers financial support to organizations that provide women with alternatives to abortion. Its publications include the quarterly *Human Life Review* and books and pamphlets on abortion, bioethics, and family issues.

Human Life International (HLI)
4 Family Life Ln., Front Royal, VA 22630
(540) 635-7884 • fax: (540) 635-7363
e-mail: hli@hli.org • website: www.hli.org

HLI is a pro-life family education and research organization that opposes abortion. It offers positive alternatives to what it calls the antilife/antifamily movement. The organization publishes *Confessions of a Prolife Missionary*, *Deceiving Birth Controllers*, and the monthly newsletters *HLI Reports* and *Special Reports*.

National Abortion and Reproductive Rights Action League (NARAL)
1156 15th St. NW, Suite 700, Washington DC 20005
(202) 973-3000 • fax: (202) 973-3096
e-mail: naral@naral.org • website: www.naral.org

NARAL works to develop and sustain a pro-choice political constituency in order to maintain the right of all women to legal abortion. The league briefs members of Congress and testifies at hearings on abortion and related issues. It publishes the quarterly *NARAL Newsletter.*

National Coalition of Abortion Providers (NCAP)
206 King St., Alexandria, VA 22314
(703) 684-0055 • fax: (703) 684-5051
e-mail: ronncap@aol.com • website: www.ncap.com

NCAP is a pro-choice organization that represents the political interests of independent abortion providers nationwide. The coalition lobbies in Washington, DC, for pro-choice, pro-provider policies. NCAP publishes the bimonthly newsletter *NCAP News*.

National Conference of Catholic Bishops (NCCB)
3211 Fourth St. NE, Washington, DC 20017-1194
(202) 541-3000 • fax: (202) 541-3054
website: www.nccbusc.org

The NCCB, which adheres to the Vatican's opposition to abortion, is the American Roman Catholic bishops' organ for unified action. Through its committee on pro-life activities, it advocates a legislative ban on abortion and promotes state restrictions on abortion, such as parental consent/notification laws and strict licensing laws for abortion clinics. Its pro-life publications include the educational kit *Respect Life* and the monthly newsletter *Life Insight*.

National Right to Life Committee (NRLC)
419 Seventh St. NW, Suite 500, Washington, DC 20004
(202) 626-8800
e-mail: nrlc@nrlc.org • website: www.nrlc.org

NRLC is one of the largest organizations opposing abortion. The committee campaigns against legislation to legalize abortion. It encourages ratification of a constitutional amendment granting embryos and fetuses the same right to life as living persons, and it advocates alternatives to abortion, such as adoption. NRLC publishes the brochure *When Does Life Begin?* and the *National Right to Life News*.

Planned Parenthood Federation of America (PPFA)
810 Seventh Ave., New York, NY 10019
(212) 541-7800 • fax: (212) 245-1845
e-mail: communication@ppfa.org
website: www.plannedparenthood.org

PPFA is a national organization that supports people's right to make their own reproductive decisions without governmental interference. It provides contraception, abortion, and family planning services at clinics located throughout the United States. Among its extensive publications are the pamphlets *Abortions: Questions and Answers*, *Five Ways to Prevent Abortion*, and *Nine Reasons Why Abortions Are Legal*.

Pro-Life Action League (PLAL)
6160 N. Cicero Ave., Suite 600, Chicago, IL 60646
(773) 777-2900 • fax: (773) 777-3061
e-mail: scheidler@ibm.net • website: www.prolifeaction.org

PLAL is a pro-life organization dedicated to ending abortion. Working through nonviolent direct action—particularly sidewalk counseling—the league actively protests abortion. Its website contains press releases related to PLAL's current campaigns and its efforts to maintain protesters' access to abortion clinics. Its student research section includes the articles "Back Alley Abortion" and "Sidewalk Counseling."

Religious Coalition for Reproductive Choice (RCRC)
1025 Vermont Ave. NW, Suite 1130, Washington, DC 20005
(202) 628-7700 • fax: (202) 628-7716
e-mail: info@rcrc.org • website: www.rcrc.org

RCRC consists of more than thirty Christian, Jewish, and other religious groups committed to helping individuals make decisions concerning abortion in accordance with their conscience. The organization supports abortion rights, opposes anti-abortion violence, and educates policy makers and the public about the diversity of religious perspectives on abortion. RCRC publishes booklets, an education essay series, the pamphlets *Abortion and the Holocaust: Twisting the Language* and *Judaism and Abortion*, and the quarterly *Religious Coalition for Reproductive Choice Newsletter*.

Bibliography of Books

Randy Alcorn — *Prolife Answers to Prochoice Arguments.* Sisters, OR: Multnomah, 2000.

Linda J. Beckman and S. Marie Harvey, eds. — *The New Civil War: The Psychology, Culture, and Politics of Abortion.* Washington, DC: American Psychological Association, 1998.

James F. Bohan — *The House of Atreus: Abortion as a Human Rights Issue.* Westport, CT: Praeger, 1999.

Leslie Bonavoglia, ed. — *The Choices We Made: Twenty-five Women and Men Speak Out About Abortion.* New York: Four Walls Eight Windows, 2001.

Mary Boyle — *Rethinking Abortion: Psychology, Gender, Power, and the Law.* New York: Routledge, 1997.

Leslie Cannold — *The Abortion Myth: Feminism, Morality, and the Hard Choices Women Make.* Middleton, CT: Wesleyan University Press, 2001.

Kimberly J. Cook — *Divided Passions: Public Opinions on Abortion and the Death Penalty.* Boston: Northeastern University Press, 1998.

C.T. Coyle — *Men and Abortion: A Path to Healing.* Lewiston, NY: Life Cycle Books, 1999.

Daniel A. Dombrowski and Robert Deltete — *A Brief, Liberal, Catholic Defense of Abortion.* Chicago: University of Illinois Press, 2000.

Geoffrey G. Drutchas — *Is Life Sacred?* Cleveland, OH: Pilgrim, 1998.

Susan Dwyer and Joel Feinburg, eds. — *The Problem of Abortion.* Belmont, CA: Wadsworth, 1997.

David J. Garrow — *Liberty and Sexuality: The Right to Privacy and The Making of Roe v. Wade.* Berkeley: University of California Press, 1998.

Faye D. Ginsburg — *Contested Lives: The Abortion Debate in an American Community,* Berkeley: University of California Press, 1998.

Cynthia Gorney — *Articles of Faith: A Frontline History of the Abortion Wars.* New York: Simon and Schuster, 1998.

Mark A. Graber — *Rethinking Abortion: Equal Choice, the Constitution, and Reproductive Politics.* Princeton, NJ: Princeton University Press, 1996.

George Grant — *Grand Illusions: The Legacy of Planned Parenthood.* Nashville: Cumberland House, 2000.

Mary Guiden — *Partial Birth Abortion.* Denver: National Conference of State Legislatures, 1998.

Kerry N. Jacoby   *Souls, Bodies, Spirits: The Drive to Abolish Abortion Since 1973*. Westport, CT: Praeger, 1998.

Ellie Lee, ed.   *Abortion Law and Politics Today*. New York: St. Martin's, 1998.

Eileen L. McDonagh   *Breaking the Abortion Deadlock: From Choice to Consent*. New York: Oxford University Press, 1996.

Deborah R. McFarlane and Kenneth J. Meier   *The Politics of Fertility Control: Family Planning and Abortion Policies in the American States*. New York: Seven Bridges, 2000.

William F. Maestri   *Do Not Lose Hope: Healing the Wounded Heart of Women Who Have Had Abortions*. Staten Island, NY: Alba House, 2000.

Roy M. Mersky and Jill Duffy, eds.   *A Documentary History of the Legal Aspects of Abortion in the United States*. Littleton, CO: Fred B. Rothman, 2000.

Lynn Marie Morgan and Meredith W. Michaels, ed.   *Fetal Subjects, Feminist Positions*. Philadelphia: University of Pennsylvania Press, 1999.

Bernard N. Nathanson   *The Hand of God: A Journey from Death to Life by the Abortion Doctor Who Changed His Mind*. Washington, DC: Regnery, 1996.

Louis P. Pojman and Francis J. Beckwith, eds.   *The Abortion Controversy: Twenty-five Years After "Roe v. Wade": A Reader*. Belmont, CA: Wadsworth, 1998.

Suzanne T. Poppema and Mike Henderson   *Why I Am an Abortion Doctor*. Amherst, NY: Prometheus Books, 1996.

Andrea Lee Press and Elizabeth R. Cole   *Speaking of Abortion: Television and Authority in the Lives of Women*. Chicago: University of Chicago Press, 1999.

Jeffrey H. Reiman   *Abortion and the Ways We Value Human Life*. Lanham, MD: Rowman and Littlefield, 1999.

Jerry Reiter   *Live From the Gates of Hell: An Insider's Look at the Anti-Abortion Movement*. Amherst, NY: Prometheus Books, 2000.

James Risen and July L. Thomas   *Wrath of Angels: The American Abortion War*. New York: BasicBooks, 1998.

Rachel Roth   *Making Women Pay: The Hidden Costs of Fetal Rights*. Ithaca, NY: Cornell University Press, 1999.

Kathy Rudy   *Beyond Pro-Life and Pro-Choice: Moral Diversity in the Abortion Debate*. Boston: Beacon, 1996.

Jean Reith Schroedel   *Is the Fetus a Person?: A Comparison of Policies Across the Fifty States.* Ithaca, NY: Cornell University Press, 2000.

Jessica Shaver   *Gianna: Aborted . . . and Lived to Tell About It.* Colorado Springs: Focus on the Family, 1999.

Rickie Solinger, ed.   *Abortion Wars: A Half Century of Struggle, 1950– 2000.* Berkeley: University of California Press, 1998.

Raymond Tatalovich   *The Politics of Abortion in the United States and Canada: A Comparative Study.* Armonk, NY: M.E. Sharpe, 1997.

Michael Thomson   *Reproducing Narrative: Gender, Reproduction, and Law.* Brookfield, VT: Ashgate, 1998.

Georgia Warnke   *Legitimate Differences: Interpretation in the Abortion Controversy and Other Public Debates.* Berkeley: University of California Press, 1999.

Kevin Wm. Wildes and Alan C. Mitchell, eds.   *Choosing Life: A Dialogue on* Evangelium Vitae. Washington, DC: Georgetown University Press, 1997.

Index